How to fix the
PERFECT
COCKTAIL

How to fix the
PERFECT
COCKTAIL

50 *classic cocktail recipes from the world's leading bartenders*

ADAM ELAN-ELMEGIRAB

of The House of Botanicals

DOG 'n' BONE

Published in 2023 by Dog 'n' Bone Books
An imprint of Ryland Peters & Small Ltd
20–21 Jockey's Fields   341 E 116th St
London WC1R 4BW   New York, NY 10029

www.rylandpeters.com

10 9 8 7 6 5 4 3 2 1

ISBN: 978 1 912983 66 7

Printed in China

Designer: Geoff Borin
Art Director: Sally Powell
Creative Director: Leslie Harrington
Editorial Director: Julia Charles
Head of Production: Patricia Harrington
Indexer: Hilary Bird

Contents

INTRODUCTION

At the end of a long day or week it's hard to beat the ease of cracking open an ice-cold can of beer or popping a cork and pouring yourself a large glass of wine, but for me there's something all-consuming and relaxing about the process of fixing yourself a mixed drink such as a martinez, old fashioned, dry martini or daiquiri. Granted, there's a little more preparation involved when compared to opening a can or bottle, however taking a few moments to yourself, switching off all around you, and going that extra length to reward yourself with the perfect drink really elevates the experience.

The great thing with mixed drinks is their ability to suit the right taste for any occasion, whether that be a mouth-puckering pre-dinner celery sour, a refreshing bittersweet celebratory Champagne cocktail, a sessionable spiced porter sangaree or a bracingly bitter post-dinner negroni. Having been immersed in the world of cocktails for well over two decades I now have a plethora of memories where mixed drinks have been a central part of the occasion, and increasingly over the years friends and family have reached out for suggestions of what they could make for an upcoming gathering. Cocktail culture is back and it's here to stay.

Much of our personal experiences with food and drink are influenced by a range of social, political, economic, cultural and environmental factors, in this case shaping the ever-evolving cocktail culture, and so is this understanding that is the backbone of this book.

As someone who is extremely inquisitive I've long tried to understand the history and background behind cocktails and the ingredients used in them and much of that drives the way we work in our business every day. When I started out in the world of bartending back in 2001 the understanding of bitters was laughable considering their wide-scale use and importance in the history of cocktails and mixed drinks, so I set out to better figure out and appreciate what they represent. Being predominantly self taught at a time when the internet was still in its infancy, I had to go back to the beginning to gain a deep understanding and knowledge of the history of mixed drinks with the thought that it would better shape my career and the direction I wished to take it.

The Bon Vivant's Companion or How to Mix Drinks, written by Professor Jerry Thomas in 1862, is the holy grail for bartenders and drinks aficionados, being recognized as the first book ever published that had a section devoted to drinks consisting of *spirit, sugar, water and bitters* — or cocktails as they were known at the time. To this day enthusiasts seek out original copies of Thomas's book from auction sites, book stores and vintage markets in the faint hope of finding a relatively inexpensive copy. First editions of his work change hands for hundreds, if not thousands, of pounds, however most are happy to settle for a cheaper modern reprint.

Housing a collection of drink styles the tome gives over two hundred mixed drink recipes for punches, egg nogs, cocktails, juleps, smashes, cobblers, crustas, mulls, sangarees, toddies, slings, shrubs and flips, many of which are still made to this day both in their original form, or as the basis for modern adaptations. These recipes are essentially the building blocks for anyone that wishes to immerse themselves in the world of mixed drinks. Much in the same way that chefs will learn the five mother sauces, I recommend getting to grips with these families of drinks as a fundamental undertaking of learning the craft of cocktails. As soon as one understands the structure of drinks such as the Manhattan *(rye whiskey, sweet vermouth, aromatic bitters and orange curaçao)* or white lady *(dry gin,*

orange liqueur and fresh lemon juice) it becomes easier to understand the framework and links to others such as the martinez *(Old Tom gin, sweet vermouth, Boker's bitters and maraschino liqueur)* or margarita *(tequila, orange liqueur and fresh lime)*; in turn gaining a better understanding what drink style or taste would be best suited to a specific occasion.

As this book has been written to enlighten, demystify and most importantly entertain the reader about the world of mixed drinks through my own learnings, in the pages that follow I've compiled a selection of cocktails which I believe best demonstrate the role specific tastes have in beverages, so have grouped these cocktails by those five taste sensations. Bitter first and foremost, then sweet, sour, salt and umami. These are individually represented by ingredients crucial to the overall taste and flavour profile of the drink.

The recipes provided in this book are bulletproof, however it shouldn't be overlooked that taste is subjective and these formulas are simply guidelines intended to give you a framework to build drinks to suit your own tastes. Whether sour is your preference, or maybe it's sweet, a touch more strong, or stirred longer for weak, the ultimate goal is to find the perfect drink and ratio suited to your palate, so please try the recipes as provided then adjust to your desired taste preferences. Sláinte!

SCIENCE OF TASTE AND FLAVOUR

It's widely appreciated that the science behind what we taste, and our perception of flavour, is extremely complex; factoring in all five of our primary tastes; that's bitter, salt, sweet, sour and umami, and our four senses; those being what we see, hear, smell and touch. Additionally our personal understanding and appreciation of flavour is based on a whole host of variables including previous experiences: the environment, temperature, nostalgia and our general mood at the time.

Research into taste and flavour is heavily funded and ongoing with our wider understanding of both developing on a daily basis, becoming more nuanced as we delve deeper into its many complexities. Notable names such as French chemist Hervé and American author Harold McGee have written expertly and endlessly on the subject, so instead of concentrating solely on scientific study I wanted to approach this subject from a different angle, looking at things from my own personal perspective, which I believe everyone will be able to relate to and draw parallels with. I hope this will help you gain a deeper appreciation of what you like and don't like, and the reasons why that's the case. The drinks recipes in this book have also been selected and grouped for this reason with each arranged by the five primary tastes, as I'm a firm believer that flavour is very personal, continually evolving, and cannot be viewed with a one-size-fits-all ideology.

1 Apricot blossom
2 Gentain
3 Pendennis Club Cocktail *(see page 131)*
4 Apricot
5 Lime
6 Cherry

Being brought up by a Scottish mother and Middle Eastern father my appreciation for a wide range of British, Mediterranean, Arabic and Far Eastern foods developed from a very young age. For example, my tolerance of spicy foods is elevated compared to that of many of my friends who weren't introduced to spicier foods until later in life. When cooking a pot of chili for me and my wife, what I deem as very mild is abundantly hotter to her, although she is continually growing to love spicier foods, an example of our tastes changing as we age, but also a reminder that we should continually test our palates and revisit things we weren't sure of previously, so we can continue to enjoy the diversity of taste and flavour throughout our lives.

Taste

In the dedicated recipe sections that follow, I cover each of the five tastes. However, simply put, taste is what happens when our taste buds are stimulated prior to sending signals to the brain to process what is being ingested. Those tiny bumps on your tongue, collectively known as papillae, are each covered with taste buds containing the receptor cells that send those signals. Taste buds are found all over your tongue and contrary to popular belief, each taste can be detected no matter which part of the tongue comes into contact with stimuli, although certain areas do and can have larger concentrations of taste receptors.

Sight

'The first bite is with the eyes', is a well known phrase often uttered by bartenders and chefs alike and for good reason. If something isn't visually appealing it will be off-putting, but this goes further with everything we see influencing the perceived flavour. Whether it be the colour of a liquid or garnish; clarified Bloody Marys have long been developed by bartenders with guests expecting the sensation of a refreshing ice-cold drink upon being presented with a crystal clear liquid, but instead being hit with the rich mouthfeel of tomato juice and intense spices, or the shape of the vessel it's served in; there's a reason a large dram of whisky just tastes better when enjoyed from a heavy rocks glass, our eyes play a major role in our enjoyment of food and drink and in setting up our expectations.

Smell

If the first bite is with the eyes, the second is undoubtedly with the nose, with aromatics and our association with them crucial to establishing whether you will happily consume a specific foodstuff or beverage. The exact figure isn't known but it's thought around 80 per cent of flavour is unravelled by what we smell, not by what we taste, and for me aroma has always predominantly triggered memories of previous experiences, those experiences being decisive in the language we use to describe flavour. The genuine sense of puzzlement when I smell something new for the first time, searching deep into the memory bank to figure out what it reminds me of, is a wondrous thing. By the same token the aroma of food or drink that brings about memories of a negative experience, maybe food poisoning or over-indulging on a specific type of alcohol perhaps, is enough to turn your stomach.

Sound

I've long suspected the loud noise of bars and clubs impacts how a drink may taste and always maintained the perceived strength of a beverage is tempered in a noisy bar or club versus drinking the same in a quiet lounge or at home. Recent studies have backed up my suspicions with loud background noise, and drier cabin air, linked to the suppression of sweetness and saltiness in airline food, though bitter and sour flavours are largely unaffected. Umami is also heightened at altitude which may be the reason why so many are drawn to tomato juice during flights. Studies have also shown that sweetness is enhanced when combined with high-pitched sounds, and in reverse that bitterness is heightened when combined with low-pitched sound, which may go some way to explaining why whisk(e)y and rock music go together so well.

Touch

The importance of touch is no more highlighted than when considering the vessel you wish to serve a drink in. I'll be the first to admit there's something enjoyable about drinking expensive beverages from cheap reusable cups, although the experience is infinitely heightened when imbibing from the appropriate glass. An elegant Champagne coupe, vintage stemmed cocktail glass or a heavy beer tankard are all great examples of the vessel directly impacting the drink contained within, with the best example from recent memory being the glasses used at London's Bar Termini. Modelled on the type of cafe bar you'd hope to find on the streets of Italy, they serve their negronis in really delicate cocktail glasses that you feel you could easily crush between your fingers. Whether it's intentional or not, it almost serves to remind you to

be more relaxed and take a few minutes to yourself, really enjoy your drink and the surroundings, before heading back on to the bustling streets of London.

To conclude, there are many factors to consider when attempting to understand taste and flavour and our relationship with them, but as it's always evolving, it's important to understand and accept it's something we'll never fully get to grips with. Our journey with taste and flavour begins from the minute we are born right through to the day we pass and we should do all we can to make the adventure as enjoyable as possible, always striving to try something new whilst celebrating what we truly love.

AN OVERVIEW OF BITTERS AND THE COCK-TAIL

'What exactly are bitters?' is one of the most common questions I've been asked over the years and I've found no better definition than that found in, *The Standard Manual of Soda and Other Beverages: A Treatise Especially Adapted to the Requirements of Druggists and Confectioners*, first published in 1897:

'BITTERS — These are made by extracting bitter and aromatic — or bitter only — drugs with a mixture of alcohol and water; sometimes a small amount of sugar or syrup is added.'

The history of alcohol and medicine are long intertwined with almost all alcoholic products, including whisk(e)y, wine, vodka, gin, vermouth, beer and, in this case, bitters having been created and consumed for their alleged medicinal benefits and perceived health giving properties. Bitters, see also amer (French), amargo (Spanish) and amaro (Italian), are historically a type of medicine consumed for digestive purposes. You see, when you consume something bitter it stimulates the production of saliva and digestive juices within the human body, an evolutionary advancement by way of the development of bitter taste receptors which assist our bodies in recognizing the ingestion of toxic plants. Medicinal bitters were then used to improve the flavour of lesser refined wines, gins and brandies, acted as a hangover cure of sorts, and were the defining ingredient in the family of drinks known as the cock-tail.

In the seventeenth and eighteenth century, long before the word cocktail became a catch-all term for all beverages containing three or more ingredients, mixed drinks were widely recognized and grouped in families such as the sling (spirit, sugar, water), toddy (spirit, sugar, hot water), sour (spirit, sugar, citrus) or highball (single spirit and carbonated mixer). A style of drink in its own right, the cocktail is best described as:

'...a stimulating liquor, composed of spirits of any kind, sugar, water and bitters — it is vulgarly called bittered sling, and is supposed to be an excellent electioneering potion, in as much as it renders the heart stout and bold, at the same time that it fuddles the head. It is said, also to be of great use to a democratic candidate: because a person, having swallowed a glass of it, is ready to swallow any thing else.'

This was editor Harry Croswell's response to a reader enquiry asking, 'What is a cocktail?' as printed in the *The Balance and Columbian Repository* on May 13th, 1806. Simply put, the defining ingredient of a true cocktail is bitters, and the best example of a true cocktail is the old fashioned, which got its name from patrons in the latter part of the 1800s asking for a traditional, 'old fashioned cocktail', in lieu of the jazzed-up variants many bartenders were then offering.

As drink culture has continually evolved, bitters are nowadays more closely associated with the culinary world and are widely used as a flavouring extract in food and beverages, effectively acting as a spice rack for bartenders. Due to ethanol being a powerful solvent for dissolving organic compounds, this enables bartenders to mix and add flavour to drinks with ingredients that cannot be used in their original solid form.

Before we even consider the taste of bitter and how it's generally perceived when consumed, one only needs to think of the language around it and the negative connotations it conveys, understandable when you consider we have a deep-seated distaste for it from an evolutionary perspective linked to our bodies natural defence

1 Wormwood
2 Cinchona bark
3 Angelica
4 Star anise
5 Orange peel

mechanism. An adverse reaction to bitterness is at its strongest in humans whilst we are very young, as smaller doses of poisons would be required to harm or kill us, but thankfully as we age we learn to appreciate bitter tastes which explains why people generally grow to adore food and drinks such as coffee, beer, dark chocolate and alcohol, which is inherently bitter in its purest form. This learned appreciation is heightened by the fact we come to realize that bitter foods and drinks stimulate us, and in some cases are actually beneficial for our health in protecting against disease and illness. Bitter phytochemicals such as naringin (found in grapefruit), quercetin (black olives and dark chocolate) and epicatechin (blackberries and green tea) have all been shown to work as an anti-oxidant, anti-inflammatory, to reduce prostate inflammation, and to lower the risk of cancer. Research is still in its infancy but many medical professionals agree that bitter compounds have a positive effect on our health appearing to boost or enhance our systems.

Whilst our bodies may initially be telling us to avoid it, it seems the world is waking up to the joys of bitter; just look at the growing interest in craft beer and the various bitter hops brewers use, coffees which have a wide spectrum of bitter tastes dependent on the level of roast, chocolate with a higher cacao content, and cocktails which regularly use a diverse selection of bitter liqueurs and spirits.

Bitterness in what we consume is essential to balance against sweetness and I can't imagine there's a chef or bartender out there who would reject the use of bitter ingredients. They add depth and complexity but most importantly make things taste delicious.

THE ORIGIN OF BITTERS

The histories of alcohol and medicine are long intertwined with almost all alcoholic products, including whisk(e)y, wine, vodka, gin, vermouth, beer and, in this case, bitters, having been created and consumed for their alleged medicinal benefits and perceived health-giving properties. Excavations of Skara Brae in the Orkney Islands, a Neolithic settlement that was occupied from around 3180BC to 2500BC, uncovered large pottery jars which contained the remnants of an alcoholic beverage produced from oats and barley and flavoured with meadowsweet, as well as poisonous nightshade, hemlock and henbane. However, the oldest record of a medicinal alcoholic beverage dates even farther back to 7000BC in Jiahu, China, where a residue from a beverage produced from rice, honey, grapes and hawthorn fruits was discovered in 2004. Ancient Egyptians were also known to produce beer and wine, with residues of wine samples from Greece dating back to the same period of around 4000–3000BC. There is evidence of fermented horse's milk being consumed by the Mongols, mead (aka honey wine) by the Celts, and pulque from corn produced by the Mayans. As long as humans have roamed the earth we've consumed alcohol for medicinal reasons, likely discovered accidentally by eating fermented fruit. 'Let's drink to health' is one of the oldest toasts in existence and it's easy to understand why.

Adding natural botanicals, such as herbs, spices, roots and barks to alcohol created a more effective form of medicine due to the fact that the ethanol in alcohol is a powerful solvent which dissolves many organic compounds, but also acts as a means to preserve botanical matter. It is this combination of alcohol and botanicals that gave rise to the likes of vermouth, gin and bitters. The father of modern medicine, the Greek physician Hippocrates, was famed for serving his patients a wormwood wine infused with herbs and spices. This can easily be viewed as an early form of vermouth, which of course derives its name from the German word 'wermut', meaning wormwood.

While vermouth must contain wormwood to be classified as vermouth, bitters are not too dissimilar, being a more concentrated variant primarily relying on a spiritous base constructed with a variety of bittering agents. Their emergence and popularity is often lazily credited to Johann Gottlieb Benjamin Siegert of Angostura Bitters fame but they'd been around long before his time. The second man typically credited with creating bitters is the London apothecary Richard Stoughton with his *Elixir Magnum Stomachium* of 1690, also referred to as the 'Great Cordial Elixir'. I believe the confusion stems from the fact his bitters received a royal patent in 1712, the second medicine to be granted one, although there's no disputing Stoughton's marketing skills and his involvement in popularizing bitters. As drinks historian Dave Wondrich detailed to me:

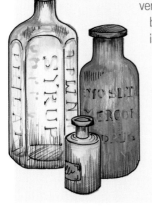

'His ads were everywhere, in all the sporting literature of the day, and he pushed his bitters as tasting good which was very important.' On top of that, he targeted his bitters as a cure for hangovers and digestive issues, two common ailments of the period, which was an unquestionable factor in his success throughout the 18th century. Despite Stoughton's role in the history of bitters he had actually followed in the footsteps of Thomas Sydenham, the true father of bitters and one of the first to champion the use of Peruvian bark, the source of quinine.

Unlike most bitters, whose primary focus was to treat ailments related to the stomach and digestion, Sydenham's Bitters were created as a cure for gout, a form of inflammatory arthritis that attacks the joints, commonly at the base of the big toe. He wrote in his *Treatise on the Gout* (1683) that '...gout generally attacks those aged persons, who have spent most of their lives in ease, voluptuousness, high living and too free an use of wine and other spirituous liquors, and at length, by reason of the common inability to motion in old age, entirely left off those exercises, which young persons commonly use.' Sydenham came to be known as the 'English Hippocrates', which is fitting as he clearly idolized Hippocrates and often referred to him in his works.

Sydenham lamented the traditional and often violent therapies of the time which included purging (removing blood) and emetics (which induced vomiting), instead recommending a gentler approach that consisted of a change in diet, regular exercise, a large intake of fluids — especially barley water which was also recommended by Hippocrates — and the consumption of his digestive medicine, Sydenham's Bitters. These were made from bitter botanicals such as angelica root, elfdock root, ground pine, wormwood leaves and centaurium, as well as antiscorbutics (medicines that counteract scurvy) such as watercress and horseradish. These bitters proved to be a popular remedy for gout, probably because they were commonly consumed by adding them to Canary wine, a sweet white wine from the Canary Islands that was extremely popular in Britain in the 17th century. Sydenham's teachings were significant in convincing many that the disease may be incurable and that the savage methods often deployed in treating it would actually aggravate the gout. Most importantly, his analytical approach developed a profile that sufferers could identify with, and the success of his bitters would see other medical practitioners attempt to imitate what Sydenham had created. With Sydenham's work the category of bitters was born...

BOTANICAL OVERVIEW

Whilst the strict definition of botanicals refers to, 'A substance obtained from a plant and used typically in medicinal or cosmetic products', in the production of alcoholic beverages, in this case bitters, we are referring to the ingredients utilized in a specific recipe to impart flavour, most commonly herbs, spices, roots and barks. With the wealth of brands and products available, and the main focus being on flavouring and not alleged medicinal benefits, the range of botanicals employed nowadays goes far beyond classic options with tea, coffee, chocolate, coconut, pineapple, maple, pecan nut, cucumber and even pumpkin now in some formulations.

Bittering Agents

Primarily roots and barks, but not exclusively, these offer varying degrees of taste and flavour with their main inclusion to impart bitterness though the flavour of the likes of dandelion root, wild cherry bark and rhubarb root is also desirable when considering the final flavour profile.

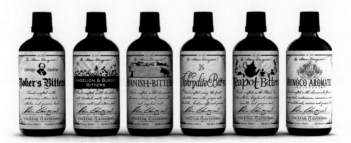

1 Quassia plant
2 Apothecary bottle
3 Angelica root

Angelica Root

Angelica archangelica

Apiaceae

A historic remedy for digestive problems and used widely in perfumery as an aroma fixative, the stems and dried roots of angelica have long been used to flavour bitters and liqueurs and is one of the key botanicals found in many gins. The long, thick twisted roots have an unmistakable earthy aroma, almost musk like, with a woodsy bittersweet taste.

Cinchona Bark

Cinchona succirubra

Rubiaceae

Arguably the most consumed bitter botanical in the world today, cinchona bark is widely coveted for its extract quinine that is used in the production of bitters, spirits, liqueurs, fortified and aromatized wines and most famously, tonic water, which was likely created as a means to temper the bitterness of the drug. An effective curative and preventative for malaria, at its height in the 1800s the British Empire were using over 700 tons of the bark every year. Sourcing cinchona and quinine in the UK today is extremely difficult unless prescribed by a doctor, which it often is to deal with leg cramps. Caution is advised when handling cinchona as its twenty three species each contain varying levels of quinine. To taste on its own it is very, very bitter and jarring to the palate.

Treacle, *see p.96*

Angostura Bark

Cusparia febrifuga

Rutaceae

Historically used by the natives of South America for its medicinal properties, at the time of writing over-harvesting of angostura bark has made it very difficult to obtain, though it should be noted its pungent aroma and flavour aren't necessarily desirable if intending to use on their own. It is no surprise that recipes for angostura-style bitters from the 1800s, when they were used to treat fever, dysentery and digestive ailments, were used in tandem with other bitter botanicals and a vast array of flavoursome spices such as cinnamon, cloves, nutmeg, cardamom and ginger.

Ol' Dirty Bastard, *see p.74*

Dandelion Root

Taraxacum officinalis

Asteraceae

One of the more delicious smelling and tasting bitter roots, dandelion is bittersweet with a flavour not too dissimilar to mild coffee, with the root often ground down and used to produce a coffee-like beverage. Native to Europe and Asia, it now grows around the globe in the likes of Russia, USA and Canada. Its most famous usage is in tandem with burdock root in dandelion & burdock, originally a fermented drink like beer or mead (honey wine) but now most commonly a type of flavoured soda. It is still widely used for its proven medicinal properties.

Autumn Negroni, *see p.154*

Gentian Root

Gentiana lutea

Gentianaceae

Up there in the debate with cinchona for most widely used bitter plant in the world, gentian is the key bittering agent in the most famous bitters of them all, Angostura, but is also frequently used in a wide number of bitter liqueurs and amaro such as the Italian Campari, and the French Suze, Amer Picon, Salers and Aveze. The English botanist Nicholas Culpeper spoke fondly of gentian, saying, 'it comforts the heart and preserves it from fainting and swooning'. Taking its name from the King Gentius of Greece, it has been used medicinally for a few thousand years. As the most bitter plant on earth a little goes a long way, likely explaining why it's used by so many, though the fact it tastes delicious, starting sweet before finishing intensely bitter, helps as well. It's probably my favourite bittering agent.

Quassia Bark

Quassia amara

Simaroubaceae

Gaining its name from the eighteenth century Surinamese botanist Graman Quasi, who used the bark to treat patients suffering from fevers, quassia bark is still used as an effective anti-malarial and in the production of shampoo to combat head lice. Native to the tropical regions of the Americas and Caribbean, its bitter qualities are utilized today in the manufacture of food and drink, and it's the chief bittering agent in Boker's bitters, both historically and in my modern reformulation. The bitterness imparted by quassia is very sharp and almost astringent, requiring an element of skill to obtain the right balance as too much can really throw a recipe.

Hops

Humulus lupulus

Cannabaceae

One of the preeminent ingredients used today in the production of beer, which itself dates back around 9000 years, the first recorded history of hops being used in the manufacture of beer dates to 822 AD where it started to be used as a flavouring and preservative. Prior to the introduction of hops, brewers would use all manner of botanicals to flavour and preserve their beers, with the combination being referred to as, 'grut' or 'gruit'. Hop bitters, in the original style of medicinal bitters, could be found in the 18th and 19th centuries though the first use I'm aware of in the modern cocktail bitters market was in Bittermens sensational Hopped Grapefruit Bitters. With dozens of hop varieties out there the potential flavour profiles range from piney to citrus, earthy to spicy.

Lady Colombia, *see p.111*

Rhubarb Root

Rheum officinale

Polygonaceae

While it is the tart stalks of rhubarb we're all accustomed to, thanks to desserts such as rhubarb crumble, with its unmistakable oversized leaves being poisonous, it is the root of rhubarb which is called for in the production of bitters and has a long history of usage in medicine primarily as a laxative and digestive aid. The flavour of the root is unique, being both sour and bitter upon tasting. For me it has similar taste and aromatics not too far away from vinegars and I've always wanted to dabble with the root in the production of shrubs, an incredibly refreshing American colonial drink that combines vinegar, fruit and sugar.

Wormwood

Artemisia absinthium

Asteraceae

It's been used in the production of wines and spirits for thousands of years, it has been known to take the place of hops in beer, vermouth takes its name for the German word for it (*vermut*), and it's a principle flavour in absinthe, which was wrongly blamed for causing many of French society's ills in the late 1800 and early 1900s leading to an almost century-long ban based solely on conjecture. Wormwood does contain the toxic compound thujone, but modern scientific research conducted on pre-ban absinthe found such minute traces make its way into your glass that it's not worth worrying about. Put it this way, by the time you consumed enough to actually cause harm you'd long be dead from alcohol poisoning. Another sharp bittering agent, its menthol-like aromatics and herbal taste lend it to pair magnificently well with the likes of fennel, anise and caraway seeds.

Bijou, *see p.70*

Pendennis Club Cocktail,
see p.131

Wild Cherry Bark

Prunus serotina

Rosaceae

Ever wondered why many cough syrups and throat lozenges
are cherry flavoured? Well now you know. Though some modern
medicines may not explicitly use wild cherry bark in their
formulations, many companies such as Vicks still do due to its ability
to treat coughs and ailments including bronchitis. Also an effective
digestive aid, it's been a favourite in the world of herbal medicine for
hundreds of years, though its flavour makes it appealing to food and
drinks manufacturers as well, with pleasant aromatics and an earthy
cherry flavour dominant.

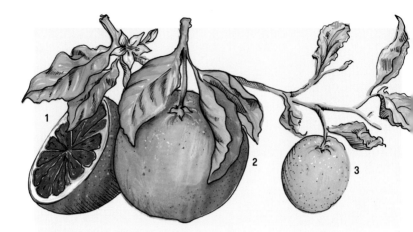

1 Blood orange
2 Pink grapefruit
3 Persian lime

Citrus Fruits

Though typically associated with the taste sensation of sour, the oils and pith found on citrus peels are bitter, while they also contain the flavourings of each fruit making them an ideal choice for bitters producers. Historically, the introduction of citrus and other fruit-based bitters as a dominant flavouring occurred in England in the late 1800s, prior to that they would've been used as a flavouring accent.

- Bergamot orange
- Bitter orange
- Blood orange
- Clementine
- Kaffir lime
- Key lime
- Lemon
- Mandarin
- Meyer lemon
- Persian lime
- Pink grapefruit
- Seville orange
- Tangerine
- White grapefruit

Herbs & Flowers

As with citrus fruits, dried herbs and flowers offer both subtle bitterness and complex flavour that historically was typically used to accent the dominant flavourings and back up the medicinal purpose behind the bottle, though it's not uncommon nowadays to find products that put these herbs and flowers at the forefront, again with the intended culinary use the priority.

- Chamomile flowers
- Lavender
- Lemon verbena
- Peppermint
- Rosemary
- Spearmint

1 Peppermint
2 Chamomile flowers

Spices

The primary flavourings and most common supporting cast in bitters comes from a whole variety of spices, with familiar pairings we see in every day cooking – think fennel and anise, cinnamon and clove, or allspice and vanilla – the backbone of many products. Ideas to create your own spice mix are never far away with the likes of Middle Eastern and Far Eastern cooking reliant on complex combinations of spices. Their tried-and-tested recipes, which have been passed down over hundreds of years, should give you enough knowledge and inspiration to create a starter point to build from, or to at least understand which spices work together to enhance and complement each other.

- Allspice berries
- Anise
- Peppercorns (black, green, white, red and pink)
- Cacao nibs
- Caraway seeds

- Cardamom (black and green)
- Celery seed
- Ceylon cinnamon bark
- Cloves
- Coriander seed
- Fennel seed
- Galangal
- Ginger root
- Juniper berries
- Mace
- Nutmeg
- Red sandalwood
- Saffron
- Star anise
- Tamarind
- Vanilla pods/beans

1 Juniper berries
2 Pink peppercorns
3 Saffron

PAIRING BITTERS

While there are always exceptions when pairing bitters with specific foods and beverages, there are a few rules and guidelines worth noting that have always served me well when perfecting a recipe or looking to find the right flavour to enhance a drink. Your main objective when selecting and pairing bitters should be to complement and enhance the flavours contained within. Bitters are not intended to be the star of the show — think of them as an orchestra conductor providing direction and keeping everything balanced; and when they're not there, things can go wrong and their presence is missed.

Your attention should first focus on the ingredients a food or drink contains, and the interaction that will take place when combining its primary taste with bitterness, because salt, sweet, sour and umami each interact with bitterness in a unique way. I've further detailed this in the recipe section, with each drink showcasing the interaction, but the following general rules apply.

When I started producing bitters in 2009, I was the first bitters brand in history to break with convention and openly discuss the botanical formulation and list the ingredients on the bottle. This stemmed from my background working as a bartender and desiring to know every small detail about the products I worked with. Being largely secretive, bitters companies were never open about what their products contained, which at first made my job purely guesswork, so I wanted to adopt a different approach and to better arm bartenders and consumers with the information they required to make informed choices. As an example, orange bitters work wonderfully well in both dry gin martinis and sweet rye Manhattans, though in my personal opinion a sweeter orange bitters such as Angostura lends itself better to a gin-based drink, the bittersweet orange notes pairing wonderfully with the common botanicals in gin and the dry vermouth, while spicier orange bitters such as Regans' No. 6 better suits the coffee, chocolate, vanilla and pepper in the whiskey, as well as the dried-fruit flavours of sweet vermouth.

Bitter combined with other bitters will lengthen and accentuate bitterness

Sour will be dulled but can temper the taste of bitterness

Sweet can be used to suppress, or can be suppressed by the addition of, bitterness

Umami will heighten other flavours while suppressing bitterness

Salt suppresses bitterness

If I were to use Tanqueray 10 gin, which contains both chamomile and grapefruit, in a dry martini, I may wish to enhance the chamomile and introduce a secondary citrus note, leaving out classic orange bitters and using my own Spanish bitters, which call for chamomile flowers, lemon peel and orange peel. This would take the drink down a more floral and citrus route. However, if I wanted to highlight the grapefruit, in which case Bittermens' Hopped Grapefruit Bitters would be perfect. For the rye Manhattan, the warm baking spices such as cinnamon and allspice are great with orange bitters, but should I want something a bit richer and more indulgent, I might opt for a complementary chocolate bitters, or a coffee bitters, or a chocolate and coffee bitters, such as my Aphrodite bitters.

If the objective was to enhance those baking spices, then a classic aromatic bitters such as Angostura, Orinoco, Boker's, Amargo Chuncho or Abbotts would do the trick. Each of these again works brilliantly with the dried-fruit flavours in the vermouth as well, though you could focus on the dried fruit instead and bring in a cherry bitters, or a plum bitters, or even an apricot bitters. As with all combinations and pairings, it's all about complementing and enhancing. Look at your base spirit and other key ingredients, take note of the key flavourings, or botanicals in the case of gin, and pair those flavours with an appropriate bitters that will result in a drink focused on your desired or favoured flavour profile.

BAR TOOLS

With the growing consumer interest in cocktails, coupled with the re-emergence of the career bartender, the wealth and breadth of readily available drinks; making equipment sees many furniture and homeware stores stocking cocktail tools alongside those that were previously aimed solely at chefs and home cooks. The ease with which the following pieces of equipment can be obtained is literally at the click of a mouse.

Bar spoons: a metal spoon which typically has a long spiral handle. A chopstick can be used if you have difficulty handling a barspoon

Bitters bottles: not a necessity for the home bartender as all bitters brands come with a dasher top and/or pipette but should you want uniformity across the size of dash you can decant into a separate dasher bottle

Cocktail shaker: the classic Boston shaker, the combination of metal and glass halves, is now commonly usurped by metal on metal shakers, two-piece Parisienne shakers, and three-piece Cobbler shakers. The type you wish to use will solely be down to availability and personal preference

Champagne stopper: you'll need one of these if you don't drink Champagne fast enough!

Channel knife: to be used with fruits and vegetables to make spirals for garnishing

Citrus press: AKA a Mexican elbow, these are available in different sizes dependent on the citrus fruit it is to be used. One large enough for lemons and limes and a second large enough for orange and grapefruit will suffice

Chopping Board: AKA a small cutting board, for preparing various garnishes

Digital scales: for weighing and measuring ingredients in the preparation of housemade syrups and suchlike

Fine strainer: AKA a tea strainer, for removing fine detritus and chips of ice from shaken drinks

Funnel: you'll require one to transfer the likes of homemade syrups into clean glass bottles

Grater: for citrus zest and spices such as cinnamon or nutmeg

Hawthorne strainer: the most recognizable strainer, used in conjunction with your cocktail shaker (and fine strainer) to hold back large pieces of ice and ingredient debris you have shaken your drink with

Ice scoop: so you don't have to use your hands to transfer ice from your freezer

Jiggers 25/50 ml or 1/2 oz: a double-sided measure

Julep strainer: used in conjunction with you mixing glass to hold back cubes of ice

Knives: for cutting fruit, vegetables and preparing garnishes

Lewis bag: to be filled with cubed ice and used in conjunction with a wooden mallet to make cracked and crushed ice (alternatively you can wrap ice cubes in a clean kitchen towel)

Mallet: to be used in conjunction with a Lewis Bag to make cracked and crushed ice

Measuring jug/pitcher: for measuring larger volumes of liquid, notably in the preparation of homemade syrups and fresh pressed juices

Measuring spoons: for measuring smaller volumes of liquid, notably in the preparation of drinks calling for rich and bold ingredients that require careful handling to ensure balance is maintained

Mixing glass: the glass half of a Boston shaker can suffice though it is worth investing in a larger mixing glass to prepare all stirred drinks

Muddler: for pressing fruit, herbs and spices when preparing a drink, a rolling pin will suffice, though the use of muddlers has decreased in recent years as bartenders opt to use fresh squeezed in lieu of muddled citrus

Pour spouts: not a necessity for the home bartender but if you're making large numbers of drinks they are worth investing in

GLASSWARE

Your serving vessel of choice is as important as the ingredients within a mixed drink, including any potential garnish, with each contributing to our first impressions whilst also setting up our expectations for the drink contained within. Selected vessels will also impact on the aromatics, taste and flavour depending on their shape. The range of glassware available nowadays is expansive so the style you ultimately go for will be purely down to personal aesthetics though I have offered some suggestions that cover each drink in this book, along with the approximate size required.

Cocktail (150 ml/5 oz): most commonly associated with the 'V' shaped glass made iconic by the martini, which I personally hate as they are a nightmare to hold, visits to antique stores will turn up an incredible selection though I highly recommend the Nick & Nora style glass for its bulbous shape that's not as shallow as a coupette.

Coupe (180 ml/6 oz): commonly used in favour over 'V' shaped martini glasses in bars nowadays, the Champagne coupe is also the glass of choice for a number of wine sommeliers who champion it in place of the flute.

Goblet (300 ml/10 oz): a footed glass or chalice which can be substituted for a large wine glass.

Flute (240 ml/8 oz): long-stemmed fluted glass.

Punch bowl (various): a serving bowl which can hold a large block of ice as well as the punch, used in conjunction with a ladle and cups. The required size will solely depend on how many people you wish to serve.

Rocks (360 ml/12 oz): a short tumbler most commonly used for serving spirits such as whisky on the rocks (over ice), these come in various sizes but it is essentially a double rocks you'll require for cocktails served in this type of glass.

Highball (300 ml/10 oz): a large thin glass or tumbler which some often refer to as a Collins glass, probably best well known as the vessel most bars will serve a gin & tonic.

Wine glass (360 ml/12 oz): stemmed glassware that comes in a range of sizes, styles and shapes.

TECHNIQUES

The preparation methods of the 50 drinks featured in this book are all straight-forward, being only shaken, stirred, thrown or swizzled, with any additional groundwork relating to the manufacture of a specific ingredient such as a syrup or in readying a garnish. Every recipe has precise directions of how to produce them detailed, though further general information can be found below.

Setting up

Ensure all your glassware has been cleaned and polished before making any drink. If space allows, all glassware should be chilled in a fridge or freezer before making any drink. Alternatively you can fill the glass with crushed ice to chill as and when a glass is needed. Cocktails that require a sugar or salt rim, such as the A Beer and a Smoke (see page 112), should have the rim added prior to chilling though take into account the method of chilling with crushed ice is not desirable with rimmed drinks.

Stirring

Ensure all required ingredients are at hand. For stirred drinks you will add all the ingredients to your mixing glass before filling around three quarters of the way full with cubes of ice. Slide your bar spoon in between the ice and glass then stir for approximately 15–20 seconds or, as a rule of thumb, until the level of liquid and ice are equal. How long is actually required will depend on how dry your ice is at the beginning of the stirring process, for example if you have taken ice straight out the freezer you may need to stir for longer or add a splash of water. Before straining into your chilled glass it is worth tasting the drink to ensure it has been diluted and chilled enough, should you feel it needs longer add some more cubes of ice and stir for a few more seconds. To strain, place a julep strainer on top of the ice and pour the drink through the strainer into your chilled glassware.

Should a drink call for bitters or a rich herbal liqueur such as Green Chartreuse, you may want to add these first to ensure you have added the correct amount, so it doesn't throw the balance of a drink if you've accidentally added too much.

Shaking

Ensure all required ingredients are at hand. As with stirred drinks you will add all ingredients to one half of your shaker, then fill with ice, cap with the other half, and shake hard for approximately 10 seconds or until the cocktail shaker is shockingly cold. Again, how long is actually required will depend on how dry your ice is. To strain the drink after shaking, place a Hawthorne strainer over the top of the shaker containing the shaken drink and pour. Should you have added fresh squeezed juices or other solid ingredients such as spices or herbs you will want to pass the drink through a fine strainer when pouring into your chilled glassware to extract all detritus.

If the drink's ingredients contain fresh egg whites, milk or cream, you will want to use a technique referred to as dry shaking, that's first shaking the liquid ingredients without ice for around 5 seconds to fully emulsify the various densities of liquid.

Throwing

Ensure all required ingredients are at hand. Add all ingredients to one half of your shaker, fill around three quarters full with cubed ice, then rest a julep strainer on top of the ice. Holding the shaker around head-height, pour the liquid through the ice into the second empty shaker while pulling the empty shaker away from it to aerate the drink. Pour the drink back into the shaker that contains ice and repeat the process five or six times. To finish, pour into your pre-chilled glassware or over fresh ice.

This technique is best adopted for wine based or aromatic ingredients, as well as drinks calling for tomato juice, such as the Bloody Mary (see page 140), and works perfectly with two metal shakers due to the thinner rim allowing for a tighter pour.

Swizzling

Ensure all required ingredients are at hand. Add all ingredients directly to your serving vessel, fill with crushed ice, then insert a bar spoon or swizzle stick down into the drink in the centre of the glass. Clasp your hands together with the spoon or swizzle stick in between, and rub together while occasionally moving the spoon or swizzle stick up and down to incorporate the liquid ingredients with the ice, diluting and chilling the drink, but also creating a frost on the outside of the glass. As the drink dilutes you will likely be required to add more ice, especially at the point of service. This technique works best with drinks which have a higher ABV, as the freezing point of alcohol is lower, ensuring you get the desired frost on the outside of the drinking vessel.

CHAPTER 1

BITTER
Cocktails

When bitter flavours come into contact with the human tongue it stimulates a sequence of events that culminates in the flow of digestive juices to the stomach, liver, duodenum and pancreas. This is the reason they're so heralded for their use in apéritifs, which set you up for a meal, and in digestifs, to aid digestion.

Due to the many layers of flavour they contain, bitters assist in the integration of flavour within cocktails, bridging gaps between the various components, enhancing or complementing existing flavours, and adding layers of complexity, depth and character. Bitters will temper sweetness and as detailed in William Boothby's 1908 book *World Drinks and How to Mix Them* will "remove the sharp, raw taste peculiar to all plain liquors," rounding off the edges of spirits if you must. Ultimately, as bitter is the most sensitive of tastes, the amount used in a drink will vary from person to person from those who find bitterness disagreeable, to those who actively desire it. Nonetheless, I do believe bitterness can be appreciated and enjoyed over time and will largely depend on how it's delivered, whether that's dark chocolate, a shot of espresso or a hoppy IPA.

Corn and Oil

Cocktail by Paul Lambert

The Blind Pig, Dublin, Ireland

Fresh • Spicy • Nutty

The corn and oil draws parallels with the likes of the old fashioned *(see page 66)*, with Falernum replacing sugar in the cocktail definition, and the brandy crusta *(see page 61)*, with the citrus accent softening the drink and adding an unexpected brightness.

Punchy, subtly sweet, with warm baking spices and a touch of bitterness rounding off the edges. A stunning drink.

60 ml/2 oz Gosling's Black Seal rum

22.5 ml/¾ oz Falernum

3 dashes aromatic bitters (Angostura, Bitter Truth Old Time or Dr. Adam's Orinoco)

7.5 ml/¼ oz fresh lime juice

a wedge of lime and freshly grated nutmeg, to garnish

SERVES 1

Pour all the ingredients over crushed ice in a rocks glass and swizzle *(see page 55)*. Top with more crushed ice if necessary, then garnish with a wedge of fresh lime and a hint of freshly grated nutmeg (optional).

Brandy Crusta

Cocktail by Joseph Santina

City Exchange Bar, New Orleans, USA

Bright · Aromatic · Bittersweet

The old fashioned (see page 66) is a wonderful drink, but the crusta takes things to the next level and, in my opinion, is the most overlooked family of drinks around, probably because of the preparation involved in making it. It's worth the effort though, trust me. It takes the basic DNA of the cocktail, with the addition of flavour accents by way of a touch of lemon juice and orange curaçao, the spice and vanilla typically associated with the brandy or Cognac, and a garnish unlike anything seen before. As we know, the first taste is with the eyes, and few drinks showcase this theory better, with the lemon peel and sugar crust perfectly setting you up for the drink contained within.

60 ml/2 oz brandy or Cognac

3 dashes Dr. Adam's Boker's bitters

10 ml/⅓ oz Pierre Ferrand orange curaçao

10 ml/⅓ oz fresh lemon juice

10 ml/⅓ oz Cane Sugar Syrup (see page 162)

1 lemon, to garnish

caster/superfine sugar, to garnish

SERVES 1

Start by garnishing the glass. Using a potato peeler, remove the zest from the lemon by starting at one end and winding down in a long spiral. Put the zest to one side, cut the peeled lemon in half, then rub one half round the rim of a small wine glass to moisten, before rolling the rim of the glass in sugar to form the crust. Place the glass in the fridge or freezer to chill. Add all the ingredients to a cocktail shaker, fill it with cubed ice, and shake hard for around 10 seconds. Strain into the pre-prepared cocktail glass and garnish by wrapping the lemon spiral around the inside of the glass.

Martinez/Manhattan

Unknown origin

Dark fruit · Herbal · Bittersweet

The union of spirit, vermouth and bitters has long been celebrated in the world of mixed drinks going back to the late 19th century when the forefathers of this collective, the Manhattan and the martinez, first surfaced in bar rooms in the US and across Europe. The premise is relatively simple: take a spirit, balance it with a ratio of vermouth (sweet, dry or the lesser favoured combination of the two, oddly referred to as perfect) and then finish it with bitters that will enhance and complement the base spirits.

Though it's practised less nowadays, much to my surprise as it offers up a more intriguing and complex drink, in past times bartenders would add further accents with dashes of syrups and liqueurs, such as absinthe, curaçao, maraschino and amari.

60 ml/2 oz Italian (sweet) vermouth

30 ml/1 oz The House of Botanicals Classic Old Tom gin or rye whiskey

3 dashes aromatic bitters (Angostura, Bitter Truth Old Time or Orinoco)

1 dash maraschino liqueur or orange curaçao

a cocktail cherry or lemon slice, to garnish

SERVES 1

Add all ingredients to your mixing vessel, fill with cubed ice, and briskly stir for around 15–20 seconds. Strain into a pre-chilled cocktail glass and garnish with a cocktail cherry or a lemon slice.

Kennedy Manhattan

Cocktail by Carl Wrangel

The Barking Dog, Copenhagen, Denmark

Boozy · Aromatic · Woody

The Kennedy Manhattan is a modern iteration that puts rum centre-stage with its flavours of dried fruit, warm baking spices, honey and gingerbread. This is balanced with a medium-dry vermouth based on ugni-blanc wine, which is rich in citrus, floral and fresh white fruit flavours. Adding a spoon of maple syrup adds further depth and complexity while the Boker's bitters, with its intense bitterness and pronounced smoked tea, coffee, cardamom and orange aromatics, rounds off the edges and adds to the length of the finish.

(see image on page 56)

60 ml/2 oz El Dorado 15-year-old rum

22.5 ml/¾ oz Dolin Blanc vermouth

4 dashes Dr. Adam's Boker's bitters

5 ml/1 teaspoon maple syrup

a cocktail cherry, to garnish

SERVES 1

Add all the ingredients to a mixing vessel, fill it with some cubed ice, and briskly stir for around 15–20 seconds. Strain into a pre-chilled cocktail glass and garnish with a cocktail cherry.

Flintlock

Cocktail by Tony Conigliaro

Zetter Townhouse, London, UK

Dry · Vegetal · Bitters

With a DNA similar to that of the sazerac *(see page 78)*, the end product of the Flintlock is a lot brighter and packed full of flavours you'd likely associate with England. Dry gin provides a solid base for the menthol aromatics of Fernet, and the savoury, vegetal and spiced notes of dandelion & burdock bitters.

Fernet Branca, to rinse

60 ml/2 oz Beefeater 24 gin

5 dashes Dr. Adam's dandelion & burdock bitters

15 ml/½ oz Gunpowder Tea Syrup *(see page 164)*

magician's wool, to garnish (optional)

SERVES 1

Add a large cube of ice to a rocks glass and a splash of Fernet Branca to chill and rinse. Add the gin, bitters and syrup to a cocktail shaker, fill it with cubed ice, and shake hard for 10 seconds. Discard the ice and Fernet from the glass, then fine-strain the drink into your drinking vessel. Garnish with a piece of magician's wool, if liked.

Old Fashioned

Unknown origin

Boozy · Rich · Aromatic

Quite simply, the old fashioned is an interpretation and reference to the cocktail in its purest form of spirit, sugar, water and bitters. It harks back to a period in the first Golden Age of mixed drinks where patrons would simply request a cocktail made in the old fashioned way. It is as simple as they come, but has an intrigue and ceremony around its preparation that makes it an experience comparable to the dry martini.

60 ml/2 oz bourbon, rye or aged rum

3 dashes aromatic bitters (Angostura, The Bitter Truth Old Time or Orinoco)

10 ml/⅓ oz Demerara Sugar Syrup *(see page 162)*

orange zest, to garnish

SERVES 1

Add all the ingredients to a mixing vessel, fill it with cubed ice, and briskly stir for around 15–20 seconds. Strain into an ice-filled rocks glass and garnish with a coin of fresh orange zest snapped over and dropped into the drink.

Trinidad Especial

Cocktail by Valentino Bolognese

Pura Vida, Bologna, Italy

Sharp · Green · Bittersweet

Though a rarity, larger measures of bitters have long been used in mixed drinks. Jerry Thomas' Japanese Cocktail from his 1862 bartender's guide called for half a teaspoonful of Boker's bitters, whilst Leo Engel's 1878 book *American & Other Drinks* contains three such examples, with his Swizzle, Sherry Blush and Alabazam calling for eye-opening levels of Boker's bitters and Angostura bitters respectively.

The grassy, peppery Pisco, nutty almond syrup and fresh citrus expertly temper the intensity of the bitters allowing fresh, spicy flavours to shine.

30 ml/1 oz Angostura aromatic bitters

30 ml/1 oz orgeat syrup

22.5 ml/¾ oz fresh lime juice

10 ml/⅓ oz pisco

lime zest, to garnish

SERVES 1

Add all the ingredients to your cocktail shaker, fill with cubed ice, and shake hard for around 10 seconds. Strain into a pre-chilled cocktail glass. Garnish with a spiral of lime zest.

Bijou

Cocktail by Harry Johnson

New York City, USA

Crisp · Herbal · Aromatic

Strip it down to its bare bones and the bijou is simply a riff on the original martini or martinez, with a few flavour accents and a healthy slug of Green Chartreuse added. I find the original specification from Harry Johnson, which called for equal parts gin, vermouth and Chartreuse, too heady and cloying, so I've adjusted the ratio, but not so much to mask the bold Chartreuse.

Fernet Branca, to rinse

30 ml/1 oz The House of Botanicals ABZ dry gin

30 ml/1 oz Italian (sweet) vermouth

15 ml/½ oz Green Chartreuse

1 dash absinthe

1 dash Dr. Adam's Spanish bitters or orange bitters

1 dash aromatic bitters (Angostura, Bitter Truth Old Time or Orininco)

lemon zest and a cocktail cherry, to garnish

SERVES 1

Add all ingredients to your mixing vessel, fill with cubed ice, and briskly stir for around 15–20 seconds. Strain into a pre-chilled cocktail glass and garnish with a coin of lemon zest (snapped over the drink and discarded) and a cocktail cherry.

Porter Sangaree

Cocktail by Jack McGarry

Dead Rabbit Grocery & Grog, New York, USA

Spiced · Bittersweet · Refreshing

For this drink you'll wish to use a porter or stout that offers up a base of coffee, toffee, chocolate and molasses-rich flavours. The beer is somewhat tempered but also complemented by the introduction of tangy lemon sherbet, intense warming mace and spiced aromatic bitters. A perfect warm-weather serve. For a lower ABV drink, you can use an alcohol-free porter or stout.

180 ml/6 oz porter or stout (alcohol-free if desired)

3 dashes aromatic bitters (Angostura, Bitter Truth Old Time or Orinoco)

3 dashes Mace Tincture *(see page 165)*

22.5 ml/¾ oz Lemon Sherbet *(see page 166)*

lemon zest and freshly grated nutmeg, to garnish

SERVES 1

Add all the ingredients to your mixing vessel, fill with cubed ice, and briskly stir for around 15–20 seconds. Strain into a pre-chilled cocktail glass and garnish with a coin of lemon zest (snapped over the drink and discarded) and a light dusting of freshly grated nutmeg.

Ol' Dirty Bastard

Cocktail by Bar Shira

Imperial Craft Cocktail Bar, Tel Aviv, Israel

Herbal · Vegetal · Bittersweet

You'll be hard pushed to find an apéritif- or digestif-style drink that doesn't contain some form of fortified wine, herbal liqueur, amari or bitters, and this drink is the perfect marriage of all with its combination of Italian, French and Spanish ingredients.

For an Italian bitter liqueur, amaro Montenegro leans toward the side of sweet with dominant notes of orange zest, cinnamon, ginger and vanilla, and these are perfectly complemented by the dried fruit and spice of the rich Amber vermouth. Additional depth comes by way of the vegetal, herbal and lightly spiced Cynar. The hint of Palo Cortado sherry adds a nutty, dry finish, which is lengthened by the spicy bitters, which also temper the sweet edge to the drink.

30 ml/1 oz amaro Montenegro

30 ml/1 oz amber vermouth

15 ml/½ oz Cynar

2.5 ml/½ teaspoon Palo Cortado sherry

3 dashes aromatic bitters (Angostura, Bitter Truth Old Time or Orinoco)

3 dashes Dr. Adam's dandelion & burdock bitters

SERVES 1

Add all the ingredients to your mixing vessel, fill with cubed ice, and briskly stir for around 15-20 seconds. Strain into a pre-chilled cocktail glass.

Dry Martini

Unknown origin

Dry · Crisp · Elegant

For a long time the dry martini largely omitted bitters and contained scant levels of vermouth, offering nothing more than an ice-cold glass of gin. This may be to the tastes of some, but it really does offer up an inferior cocktail when compared to one with a generous measure of vermouth and a few dashes of bitters. Thankfully the reemergence of high-quality vermouths and bitters has seen a growing trend for the true classical style.

60 ml/2 oz dry gin

15 ml/½ oz French (Dry) vermouth

3 dashes Dr. Adam's Spanish bitters or orange bitters

lemon zest, to garnish

SERVES 1

Add all the ingredients to your mixing vessel, fill with cubed ice, and briskly stir for around 15–20 seconds. Strain into a pre-chilled cocktail glass and garnish with a coin of lemon zest snapped over the drink and discarded.

Sazerac

Unknown origin

Boozy · Aromatic · Bittersweet

Despite the fact the cocktail had been defined in print 32 years earlier, the Sazerac company maintain this was the world's first cocktail created in 1838. The story goes that New Orleans apothecary Antonie Amedie Peychaud would treat friends to his brandy toddy recipe which contained the medicinal Peychaud's bitters. These toddies were made using a measuring cup called a coquetier, which the word cocktail is also alleged to have derived from. To quote Mark Twain, "Never let the truth get in the way of a good story."

60 ml/2 oz VSOP Cognac

4 dashes Peychaud's bitters

10 ml/⅓ oz Cane Sugar Syrup
(see page 162)

3 dashes absinthe

lemon zest, to garnish

SERVES 1

Add the first three ingredients to your mixing vessel, fill it with cubed ice, and briskly stir for around 25–30 seconds. Add the absinthe to a pre-chilled rocks glass to coat the inside, then strain the drink into it. Garnish with a coin of lemon zest snapped over the drink and then discarded.

Queen's Park Special

Unknown

Queen's Park Hotel, Port of Spain, Trinidad

Fresh · Bright · Aromatic

Though it's not as well known as its cousin, the Queens Park Swizzle, I found this drink referenced in Harper's Bazaar from 1941 and it's well worth your attention, with it utilizing the lighter butterscotch, cocoa and vanilla notes of Trinidadian rum. The introduction of falernum adds a layer of sweetness, spice and freshness, with the bitters adding length and depth.

60 ml/2 oz Angostura 1919 rum

30 ml/1 oz falernum

4 dashes aromatic bitters (Angostura, Bitter Truth Old Time or Orinoco)

30 ml/1 oz fresh lime juice

22.5 ml/¾ oz Demerara Sugar Syrup *(see page 162)*

fresh mint, to garnish

SERVES 1

Pour all the ingredients into an ice-filled highball glass, fill it with crushed ice, and swizzle *(see page 55)*. Top with more crushed ice and garnish with a sprig of fresh mint.

Gin Pahit

Unknown origin

Dry · Bitter · Aromatic

Sugar is not a standard requirement in classic pink gin or gin pahit, but I've found it to be preferable for those who are feeling adventurous and testing the water. Hot, spicy and bracing, it's not for everyone, but delightful to a few.

45 ml /1 ½ oz navy-strength gin

15 ml/½ oz aromatic bitters (Angostura, Bitter Truth Old Time or Orinoco)

5 ml/1 teaspoon Cane Sugar Syrup *(see page 162)*

lemon zest and (optional) pickled onions, to garnish

SERVES 1

Add all the ingredients to your mixing vessel, fill it with cubed ice, and briskly stir for around 15–20 seconds. Strain into a pre-chilled cocktail glass and garnish with a coin of fresh lemon zest and, optionally, onions pickled in chilli vinegar served on the side.

Tuxedo

Harry MacElhone

Harry's New York Bar, Paris, France

Herbal · Stoned fruit · Bittersweet

Fundamentally a riff between the original martini and dry martini with sweet and dry ingredients crucial to the drink's success. Lightly sweetened Old Tom gin helps amplify flavour, with the accents of maraschino, absinthe and orange bitters bringing further delicious noise.

45 ml/1½ oz The House of Botanicals Classic Old Tom gin

45 ml/1½ oz French (dry) vermouth

3 dashes Dr. Adam's Spanish bitters or orange bitters

1 dash maraschino liqueur

1 dash absinthe

lemon zest, to garnish

SERVES 1

Add all the ingredients to your mixing vessel, fill it with cubed ice, and briskly stir for around 15–20 seconds. Strain into a pre-chilled cocktail glass and garnish with a coin of lemon zest snapped over the drink and then discarded.

CHAPTER 2

SWEET
Cocktails

Unquestionably the most desired of our five tastes, human's cravings for sweetness dates back millions of years to our prehistoric ancestors, as explained by Daniel Liebermann, paleoanthropologist at Harvard University, in the New York Times of June 5th 2012. "Simply put, humans evolved to crave sugar, store it and then use it. For millions of years, our cravings and digestive systems were exquisitely balanced because sugar was rare. Apart from honey, most of the foods our hunter-gatherer ancestors ate were no sweeter than a carrot. The invention of farming made starchy foods more abundant, but it wasn't until very recently that technology made pure sugar bountiful."

Also being stored as fat, ergo storing energy, eating sugar would have been a way to prevent starvation when sugar was scarce. Things are very different nowadays with it present in nearly everything we consume. Additionally the consumption of sugar activates the brain's reward system, releasing dopamine.

Sugar's role in drinks is primarily as a carrier, helping to build layers of flavour on our palates whilst also counterbalancing bitter and sour. This is best showcased when you add a dash of sweet to stirred drinks which are quite dry, for example a dry martini *(see page 77)* will have its flavour heightened with a dash of sweet orange curaçao, maraschino liqueur or honey.

Nordic Club

Author's own

Fresh · Fruity · Complex

Native to Scandinavia, akvavit is a flavoured spirit distilled from potatoes or grain with a predominant flavour of caraway, the warm, nutty, aromatic split halves of dried fruit from the caraway plant, backed up by a host of other botanicals such as lemon, star anise, fennel, dill, cloves and cardamom. Used in scant quantities it can offer similar properties to the likes of dry vermouth when offering balance to a drink. The general formulas of the clover and Nordic club are very similar though there is a more prevalent warming character in the latter, with the ginger, anise and orange in dandelion and burdock bitters working in tandem with the profile of the akvavit to offer a more autumnal quality.

4 fresh raspberries

45 ml/1½ oz ABZ dry gin or Everleaf Mountain (alcohol-free)

15 ml/½ oz Aalborg Taffel akvavit

1 dash Dr. Adam's dandelion & burdock bitters

22.5 ml/¾ oz fresh lemon juice

15 ml/½ oz Cane Sugar Syrup *(see page 162)*

15 ml/½ oz fresh egg white

SERVES 1

Add all the ingredients to a cocktail shaker, quickly dry-shake, then fill with cubed ice, and shake hard for around 10 seconds. Strain into a pre-chilled cocktail glass.

Añejo Highball

Cocktail by Dale DeGroff

Rainbow Room, New York City, USA

Fresh · Spiced · Citrus

The Añejo Highball is unquestionably one of DeGroff's most well-known drinks, created in 1990 as a tribute to Cuban bartenders whilst he was consulting for Angostura Bitters. The addition of orange curaçao, think notes of zesty orange, cinnamon, marmalade and black pepper, really elevates this serve and confirms Dale's genius.

45 ml/1½ oz Añejo rum or Everleaf Forest (alcohol-free)

15 ml/½ oz orange curaçao

15 ml/½ oz fresh lime juice

60 ml/2 oz ginger beer

2 dashes Dale DeGroff's pimento bitters

lime and orange slices, to garnish

SERVES 1

Build all the ingredients in an ice-filled highball glass, lightly stir, and garnish with a slice each of fresh lime and fresh orange.

Fosbury Flip

Author's own

Spiced · Rich · Moreish

Flips as we know them nowadays are a mix of whole raw eggs, spirit, sugar and spices, if you must, a more elegant take on festive egg nog, which also includes cream. The combination of sweet and spicy Drambuie, the tropical and dried fruits in the rum, spiced chocolate bitters, and the accents of salt and pepper, all bound together in the beaten egg make for a truly wonderful take on a personal favourite family of drinks.

1 barspoon caraway seeds

60 ml/2 oz Drambuie

30 ml/1 oz aged rum

2 dashes Xocolatl mole bitters

1 large free-range egg

5 ml/1 teaspoon Cane Sugar Syrup *(see page 162)*

1 grind rock salt

1 grind black pepper

freshly grated nutmeg, to garnish

SERVES 1

Muddle the caraway seeds in the base of a cocktail shaker, add the liquor, and steep for 2 minutes. Add the remaining ingredients, quickly dry-shake, then fill with cubed ice and shake hard for a further 10 seconds. Strain into a pre-chilled goblet, then garnish with a dusting of freshly grated nutmeg.

Florabotanica

Cocktail by Jason Williams

Proof & Co., Singapore

Floral · Aromatic · Candied

In the florabotanica the addition of sweet rose syrup and dry cherry liqueur are put to great effect to balance a classic dry gin and yuzu juice; an incredibly sour and fragrant citrus fruit which is primarily cultivated in Korea, Japan and China. The liquorice flavour in the bitters, thanks to star anise, comes to the fore at the finish with a rich mouthfeel present throughout thanks to the egg white. *(see image on page 86)*

60 ml/2 oz The House of Botanicals ABZ dry gin

15 ml/½ oz yuzu juice

15 ml/½ oz rose syrup

4 dashes Dr. Adam's dandelion & burdock bitters

5 ml/1 teaspoon maraschino liqueur

15 ml/½ oz fresh egg white

a dehydrated orange wheel and edible flowers, to garnish

SERVES 1

Add all the ingredients to a cocktail shaker, quickly dry-shake, then fill with cubed ice and shake hard for around 10 seconds. Strain into an ice-filled rocks glass and garnish with a dehydrated orange wheel and edible flowers.

Aboukir Punch

Cocktail by Joseph Akhavan

Mabel, Paris, France

Boozy · Fresh · Vanilla

The Aboukir punch is a modern adaptation which stays true to the original punch formula of spirit, sugar, citrus, water and spice. The real star in this show is the infused port, with the fragrant, vanilla and sweet grassy notes of pandan proving to be an ideal partner for the woody, dark fruit flavours of the tawny port.

60 ml/2 oz Pandan-infused Tawny Port *(see page 161)*

30 ml/1 oz aged rum

30 ml/1 oz Grapefruit & Cardamom Sherbet *(see page 167)*

3 dashes Dr. Adam's teapot bitters

pan masala and a sprig of fresh mint, to garnish

SERVES 1

Build all the ingredients in an ice-filled highball glass, fill it with crushed ice, and swizzle *(see page 55)*. Top with more crushed ice and garnish with pan masala (also known as paan) and a sprig of fresh mint.

Treacle

Cocktail by Dick Bradsell

El Camion, London, UK

Fresh · Aromatic · Bittersweet

The treacle is effectively a rum old fashioned (rum, bitters, sugar) crowned with freshly pressed apple juice, with the combination of flavour giving you a drink that tastes like, well, the clue is in the name. It's just delicious.

60 ml/2 oz Gosling's Black Seal rum

2 dashes aromatic bitters (Angostura, Bitter Truth Old Time or Orinoco)

15 ml/½ oz Cane Sugar Syrup *(see page 162)*

15 ml/½ oz freshly pressed apple juice

orange zest, to garnish

SERVES 1

Add the first three ingredients to a mixing vessel, fill it with cubed ice, and briskly stir for around 15–20 seconds. Strain into an ice-filled rocks glass, top with the apple juice, and garnish with a strip of fresh orange zest snapped over and dropped into the drink.

Champagne Cocktail

Unknown origin

Clean · Crisp · Effervescent

For this recipe I've included my preferred serve for a Champagne cocktail that has the inclusion of Cognac. This style was popularized in the UK and was taught to me as being, 'the London way,' having first surfaced in the *Cafe Royal Cocktail Book*, a publication by the United Kingdom Bartender's Guild in 1937. The combination of bitters and sugar offers depth and balance to the drink, the Champagne elegant effervescence, while the Cognac adds hints of dried fruit, vanilla, nuts and spice.

1 brown sugar cube

3 dashes Peychaud's bitters

15 ml/½ oz VSOP Cognac (optional)

120 ml/4 oz Champagne

lemon zest, to garnish

SERVES 1

Place the sugar cube on a spoon, dash the bitters onto it, then drop it in the base of a Champagne flute. Add the Cognac, if using, then top with the Champagne. Garnish with a spiral of fresh lemon zest.

East India Cocktail

Unknown origin

Boozy · Tropical · Bittersweet

The East India cocktail is another great example of the continued evolution of the cocktail throughout the 19th century, with the introduction of exotic ingredients via the inclusion of pineapple syrup. The above recipe would feature in Harry Johnson's *New and Improved Bartender's Manual* of 1888, six years after his first edition was published, which strangely included the exact same drink but with raspberry syrup in place of pineapple. It is widely agreed the pineapple variant produces a superior beverage, which may explain why Johnson amended the recipe.

60 ml/2 oz VSOP Cognac

5 ml/1 teaspoon orange curaçao

3 dashes Dr. Adam's Boker's bitters

2 dashes maraschino liqueur

5 ml/1 teaspoon Pineapple Syrup *(see page 163)*

lemon zest or a cocktail cherry, to garnish

SERVES 1

Add all the ingredients to a cocktail shaker, fill it with cubed ice, and shake hard for around 10 seconds. Strain into a pre-chilled cocktail glass and garnish with a coin of fresh lemon zest or a cocktail cherry.

Montana

Unknown origin

Complex fruit · Aromatic · Herbal

In the Montana, as found in the 1900 edition of Harry Johnson's *New & Improved Bartender's Manual*, sloe gin takes centre-stage alongside dry vermouth. The aniseed and liquorice flavours found in anisette, and the citrus, perfumed and menthol notes of green cardamom, offer the crucial flavour accents required for balance.

45 ml/1½ oz sloe gin

45 ml/1½ oz French (dry) vermouth

3 dashes anisette (Arak, Ouzo or Raki)

3 dashes Scrappy's cardamom bitters

orange zest to garnish (optional)

SERVES 1

Add all the ingredients to your mixing vessel, fill it with cubed ice, and briskly stir for around 15–20 seconds. Strain into a pre-chilled cocktail glass. Garnish with a small strip of orange zest, if liked.

Hanky Spanky

Cocktail by Jack Forbes

Cloakroom Bar, Montreal, Canada

Dry · Bitter · Aromatic

The hanky spanky doesn't stray too far away from Ada Coleman's original hanky panky (pictured), but introduces deeper notes of dark fruits, cacao, coffee, chocolate and warm spices thanks to the vermouth, bitters and spicy gin, while Fernet's role is for its aromatic properties adding a fragrant, menthol note on the nose.

45 ml/1½ oz The House of Botanicals ABZ dry gin

45 ml/1½ oz Italian (sweet) vermouth

5 ml/1 teaspoon Dr. Adam's Aphrodite bitters or chocolate bitters

3 dashes Fernet Branca, to rinse

a cocktail cherry, to garnish

SERVES 1

Add the first three ingredients to a mixing vessel, fill it with cubed ice, and briskly stir for around 15–20 seconds. Strain into a pre-chilled cocktail glass which has been rinsed with the Fernet Branca. Garnish with a cocktail cherry.

CHAPTER 3

SALT
Cocktails

Salt is required by the human body and an essential part of our diets. Consisting of two electrolytes, sodium and chloride, salt helps maintain fluid balance, determining blood volume and in turn regulating blood pressure, generates nerve impulses, and assists in nutrient absorption for the likes of amino acids, chloride, glucose and water. Unlike some vitamins and minerals which are stored in the body to be used as required, we can't keep stock of salt, so when we come across it it's beneficial to eat it, which goes some way to explain why we crave it so much.

In the world of food and drink salt is somewhat the antithesis of bitterness, notably as it suppresses bitter flavours, however it performs a similar role to bitters in improving the overall taste of what it comes into contact with by heightening the flavour intensity. Salt will hide chemical or metallic off-notes, and will enhance sweetness and make sour flavours appear brighter. This is why bartenders often have a bottle of saline solution to hand, that's 10 parts water to 1 part salt, to add a few dashes to sour drinks such as a daiquiri, give life to citrus juice when it's not squeezed a la minute, or even to add a few drops to bitter drinks such as the negroni which increases the citrus flavour and the sweetness of the Campari and vermouth. Salt has often been overlooked in the world of mixed drinks but it has earned a seat at the top table, in the right hands it is an essential ingredient.

Chelsea Dove

Author's own

Bright · Clean · Fresh

Inspired by the tequila-based Paloma, this gin variant utilizes the classic style of juniper-heavy London dry gin. Working in harmony with sweet, tropical soda, brightness is introduced via a lemon sherbet, with vanilla salt adding fragrance and accentuating citrus flavours throughout. The bitters offer tea and spice notes to round off an invigorating long drink.

60 ml/2 oz dry gin or Everleaf Marine (alcohol-free)

4 dashes Dr. Adam's teapot bitters

120 ml/4 oz pineapple soda

15 ml/½ oz Lemon Sherbet (see page 166)

pinch of Vanilla Salt
(see page 169)

pineapple fronds, to garnish

SERVES 1

Build all the ingredients in an ice-filled highball glass, lightly stir, and then garnish with two pineapple fronds.

Lady Colombia

Cocktail by Alex Laurence Milia

Seed Library, London, UK

Spiced · Rich · Aromatic

With complex rum at its base, sporting myriad flavours, including chocolate, toffee, black pepper and vanilla, dry, floral vermouth provides a perfect backdrop and complements the rich sweeteners in the liqueur and maple syrup. Seasoning with cacao and coffee bitters, and warm aromatic bitters brings everything together, with the hint of salt adding a touch of elegance.

60 ml/2 oz La Hechicera rum

22.5 ml/¾ oz French (dry) vermouth

5 ml/1 teaspoon dark chocolate liqueur

5 ml/1 teaspoon maple syrup

1 dash Dr. Adam's Aphrodite bitters or chocolate bitters

1 dash Dr. Adam's Orinoco aromatic bitters

pinch of sea salt

lemon zest, to garnish

SERVES 1

Add all the ingredients to a mixing vessel, fill it with cubed ice, and briskly stir for around 15–20 seconds. Strain into an ice-filled rocks glass and garnish with a coin of fresh lemon zest snapped over and dropped into the drink.

A Beer and a Smoke

Cocktail by Jim Meehan

PDT, New York, USA

Spicy · Crispy · Invigorating

A heady take on the michelada, this adaptation does not include tomato or clamato juice, instead focusing on the citrus flavours found within, offering up a more spiritous beverage, which is complemented and tempered by the salt and sugar combination and the vegetal, savoury and herbaceous celery bitters. We recommend 4 dashes of hot sauce, but those who favour spicy foods, like myself, may be tempted to introduce more heat. To finish, the grating of fresh citrus zest is a masterstroke that adds further depth and complexity along with incredible aromatics on the nose.

30 ml/1 oz Mezcal

22.5 ml/¾ oz fresh lime juice

4 dashes hot sauce

1 dash celery bitters

6oz/180 ml pilsner beer (alcohol-free if desired)

Kosher Salt, Celery Salt, & Sugar Mix *(for rim, see page 168)*

freshly grated orange and lime zest, to garnish

SERVES 1

Add the first four ingredients to a mixing vessel, fill it with cubed ice, and briskly stir for around 15–20 seconds. Strain into a highball glass which has been rimmed with the Kosher Salt, Celery Salt, & Sugar Mix, top with the chilled beer, and garnish with freshly grated orange and lime zest.

Mexican 'Firing Squad' Special

Unknown

La Cucaracha, Mexico City, Mexico

Warm · Fruity · Aromatic

The combination of ingredients is nothing overly creative, but it's nothing short of delightful. I've adjusted the original recipe slightly to increase the sour element for modern tastes, with the bitters pairing perfectly with the tequila to pull out the warm spices like black pepper and cinnamon you expect to find. Grenadine enhances and complements the fruitiness of the spirit, and to elevate things further a few dashes of saline really takes the flavour up a notch whilst also making for a richer mouthfeel.

45 ml/1½ oz blanco tequila

22.5 ml/¾ oz fresh lime juice

15 ml/½ oz grenadine

2 dashes aromatic bitters
(Angostura, Bitter Truth Old
Time or Orinoco)

3 dashes Saline Solution
(see page 169)

a lime wedge and a cherry,
to garnish

SERVES 1

Add all the ingredients to a cocktail shaker, fill it with cubed ice, and shake hard for around 10 seconds. Strain into an ice-filled rocks glass, and garnish with a lime wedge and also a cherry.

Celery Gimlet

Cocktail by Naren Young

Dante, New York City, USA

Clean · Crisp · Vegetal

The celery gimlet combines a host of bartender favourites, such as chartreuse, elderflower liqueur and celery bitters, culminating in a supremely refreshing gimlet packed full of bright fresh herbal and vegetal flavours, the salt again elevating all the ingredients as the perfect seasoning to this incredible cocktail.

45 ml/1½ oz dry gin or Everleaf Marine (alcohol-free)

7.5 ml/¼ oz Green Chartreuse

7.5 ml/¼ oz elderflower liqueur

22.5 ml/¾ oz fresh lime juice

15 ml/½ oz Sugar Syrup
(see page 162)

15 ml/½ oz fresh celery juice

5 dashes white wine vinegar

2 dashes celery bitters

pinch of Maldon sea salt

a ribbon of celery, to garnish

SERVES 1

Add all the ingredients to a cocktail shaker, fill it with cubed ice, and shake hard for around 10 seconds. Strain into an ice-filled rocks glass and garnish with a ribbon of celery peeled using a potato peeler.

CHAPTER 4

SOUR
Cocktails

Probably the least understood of our five primary tastes, sourness is found in acidic foods containing organic acids such as malic (apples and pears), citric (lemons, limes and oranges) or ascorbic (peppers, tomatoes and broccoli). You will likely better know the latter as vitamin c, an essential nutrient responsible for the repair and growth of tissue in all parts of the human body. If you don't consume enough vitamin c you will develop scurvy, which can kill you. Thankfully citrus fruits, which are rich in vitamin c, have now been part of our diets for centuries and are key ingredients in some of the world's most famous drinks such as the daiquiri, white lady, whisk(e)y sour and margarita.

Though many fruits already contain a perfect combination of sugar and acid, hence why you can eat them in their natural state, citrus fruits have lower levels of fructose and are thus favoured in mixed drinks to counterbalance sweetness. This is why you'll see more recipes with fresh lemon and lime juice in comparison to say, orange, though a handy tip for any cocktail containing fresh orange juice is to add a few dashes of lemon to enliven the drink. Another tip for sour drinks is to add a few dashes of saline solution *(see page 169),* which again will brighten the drink and make the flavours 'pop'. Although it varies, sourness will temper the sensation of bitterness letting the other flavours in a bitters shine through.

London Calling

Cocktail by Chris Jepson

MadFox, Amsterdam, The Netherlands

Fresh · Crisp · Dry

The London calling bridges the gap between classically styled cocktails and the modern cocktail movement. The drink is perfectly balanced with the fruit and nut notes of the sherry complementing the predominant orange and spice notes offered up by the gin. Originally it was created with an orange bitters, however I often substitute it for Spanish bitters, which shares botanicals with many gins – angelica root, orange peel, coriander seed, orris root and orange peel – thus heightening and lengthening the flavour, in turn letting the base spirit shine.

45 ml/1½ oz House of Botanicals ABZ dry gin

15 ml/½ oz fino sherry

3 dashes Dr. Adam's Spanish bitters or orange bitters

15 ml/½ oz fresh lemon juice

15 ml/½ oz Cane Sugar Syrup *(see page 162)*

grapefruit zest, to garnish

SERVES 1

Add all the ingredients to a cocktail shaker, fill it with cubed ice, and shake hard for around 10 seconds. Strain into a pre-chilled cocktail glass and garnish with a coin of fresh grapefruit zest, snapped over and then dropped into the drink.

Army & Navy

Cocktail by Carroll Van Ark

PR Consultant, New York, USA

Boozy · Nutty · Fresh

A simple adaptation of a gin sour, replacing sugar with almond syrup to give it a fragrant, nutty character. The inclusion of bitters is a relatively modern adaptation that further makes the ingredients meld together and adds to the complexity of the drink. I've long believed the name holds this drink back, for it is truly delightful.

60 ml/2 oz ABZ dry gin or Everleaf Marine (alcohol-free)

2 dashes Dr. Adam's Boker's bitters

15 ml/½ oz fresh lemon juice

7.5 ml/¼ oz orgeat syrup

lemon zest, to garnish

SERVES 1

Add all the ingredients to a cocktail shaker, fill it with cubed ice, and shake hard for around 10 seconds. Strain into a pre-chilled cocktail glass and garnish with fresh lemon zest, snapped over the drink and then discarded.

Vanilla & Coconut Lassi

Author's own

Spiced · Indulgent · Bittersweet

The refreshing, sour, subtly sweet, and cooling ingredients in a Lassi make it an ideal warm weather drink, though it perfectly offsets hot spices and arguably makes a better accompaniment to hot curries than the lager most would typically go for.

60 ml/2 oz vodka or Everleaf Marine (alcohol-free)

3 dashes Dr. Adam's teapot bitters

75 ml/2½ oz coconut milk

30 ml/1 oz Greek yogurt

30 ml/1 oz Vanilla Sugar Syrup *(see page 163)*

30 ml/1 oz fresh lime juice

pinch of ground cardamom

pinch of saffron threads, plus extra to garnish

SERVES 1

Add all the ingredients to a cocktail shaker and stir thoroughly to combine before filling it with cubed ice and shaking hard for around 10 seconds. Strain into an ice-filled highball glass and garnish with a pinch of saffron threads and ground cardamom.

Pisco Sour

Unknown origin

Grassy · Tart · Spiced

Pisco is primarily centred around citrus, white pepper, vanilla and grassy notes, making for a wonderful base to add the simple sour combination of lemon and sugar. The addition of egg white tempers the bite of citrus but compensates by adding incredible mouthfeel and texture, with the foam of the egg white offering a pillow to lay the bitters atop.

60 ml/2 oz Pisco

30 ml/1 oz fresh lemon juice

15 ml/½ oz Cane Sugar Syrup
(see page 162)

15 ml/½ oz fresh egg white

3 dashes Amargo Chuncho bitters

SERVES 1

Add the first four ingredients to a cocktail shaker, fill it with cubed ice, and shake hard for around 10 seconds. Strain into a pre-chilled cocktail glass and garnish with the dashes of bitters dropped into the foam of the egg white.

Downriver

Cocktail by Liam Broom

Silverleaf, London, UK

Crisp · Tropical · Refreshing

It's the idea that flavours and aromas found within food and drink trigger our favourite memories and experiences that is partly responsible for the inclusion of the downriver, with that crisp hit of fresh honeydew melon taking me back to a hot summer's day in Ibiza lying on the beach with my wife. A complex take on the classic fizz (spirit, lemon, sugar and sparkling water), the introduction of bittersweet aperitif wine, Jasmine tea tannins and aromatic bitters offer up a refreshingly moreish drink.

30 ml/1 oz Jasmine Tea-infused Vodka
(see page 160)

22.5 ml/¾ oz Cocchi Amerlcano

30 ml/1 oz freshly pressed Honeydew melon juice

22.5 ml/¾ oz lemon juice

10 ml/⅓ oz Cane Sugar Syrup
(see page 162)

2 dashes Dr. Adam's dandelion & burdock bitters

sparkling water/soda, to top up

melon balls, to garnish

SERVES 1

Add the first six ingredients to a cocktail shaker, fill it with cubed ice, and shake hard for around 10 seconds. Prior to straining, add a splash of soda water to your tin, then strain into an ice-filled highball glass. Garnish with two melon balls.

Pendennis Club Cocktail

Unknown origin

Crisp · Citrus · Stoned fruit

Strangely it was only in recent years you could order this cocktail at the Pendennis Club following the introduction of a drink's menu showcasing the various cocktails served at the bar over the last century. The drink is primarily tart with a flavour not too dissimilar to grapefruit; subtly sweet, stoned fruit flavour throughout, and the spicy, bracing finish from the bitters. A truly exceptional cocktail that deserves more acclaim.

60 ml/2 oz ABZ dry gin

30 ml/1 oz apricot brandy

22.5 ml/¾ oz fresh lime juice

2 dashes Peychaud's bitters

a cocktail cherry, to garnish

SERVES 1

Add all the ingredients to a cocktail shaker, fill with cubed ice, and shake hard for around 10 seconds. Strain into a pre-chilled cocktail glass and garnish with a cocktail cherry.

Pegu Club

Unknown origin

Dry · Citrus · Herbal

Whether it's a drink of its climate or the ingredients of the time, the pegu club never stood out for me until I started making subtle changes to the ingredients in the original recipe. Adjusting the ratio and replacing the warm spiced notes of Angostura with cardamom bitters made every ingredient pop whilst maintaining the original beverage's style as a drier, tart cocktail.

60 ml/2 oz The House of Botanicals ABZ dry gin

22.5 ml/¾ oz orange curaçao

22.5 ml/¾ oz fresh lime juice

1 dash cardamom bitters

1 dash Peychaud's bitters

a wedge of lime, to garnish

SERVES 1

Add all the ingredients to a cocktail shaker, fill it with cubed ice, and shake hard for around 10 seconds. Strain into a pre-chilled cocktail glass and garnish with a wedge of fresh lime.

Jerez Sour

Cocktail by Katie Nelson

The Columbia Room, Washington DC, USA

Nutty · Aromatic · Citrus

Influenced by the Japanese cocktail (brandy, orgeat, lemon juice and Boker's bitters), the Jerez sour was created to pair with crispy pig's head croquettes from The Columbia Room's bar menu. The drink adds tartness to cut through the fat of the croquette, whilst also adding a richness and subtle sweetness that would complement the rich toasted chestnut flavour in the dish.

45 ml/1½ oz brandy de Jerez

22.5 ml/¾ oz fresh lemon juice

22.5 ml/¾ oz orgeat syrup

1 dash Dr. Adam's Boker's bitters

15 ml/½ oz dry oloroso sherry (float)

orange zest and a cocktail cherry, to garnish

SERVES 1

Add all the ingredients to a cocktail shaker, fill it with cubed ice, and shake hard for around 10 seconds. Strain into a pre-chilled cocktail glass and garnish with a speared twist of fresh orange zest and a cocktail cherry.

Hemingway Daiquiri
(aka Papa Doble)

Cocktail by Constantino Ribalaigua Vert

La Floridita, Havana, Cuba

Dry · Fresh · Crisp

The Papa Doble was a double daiquiri created for Ernest Hemingway, or Papa as he was affectionately termed, comprising almost 120 ml/4 oz light rum, around a teaspoon of maraschino liqueur, the juice of two whole limes and half a grapefruit, before being blended with ice. I've halved that recipe for reasons which really shouldn't need explaining, opted to shake it with ice, and added just a hint of tart grapefruit bitters.

60 ml/2 oz light rum

10 ml/⅓ oz maraschino liqueur

2 dashes grapefruit bitters

15 ml/½ oz fresh pink grapefruit juice

15 ml/½ oz fresh lime juice

15 ml/½ oz Cane Sugar Syrup
(see page 162)

a wedge of lime, to garnish

SERVES 1

Add all the ingredients to a cocktail shaker, fill it with cubed ice, and shake hard for around 10 seconds. Strain into a pre-chilled cocktail glass and garnish with a wedge of fresh lime.

Dr. Cocktail

Unknown origin

Spiced · Fresh · Aromatic

This adaptation of the Dr. cocktail is more complex than its original guise; rich, spicy, funky and packed full of the hogo you expect to find in Jamaican rum and Swedish punsch, rounded off with the dry, spicy, oaked bitters.

45 ml/1½ oz aged rum

22.5 ml/¾ oz Swedish punsch

22.5 ml/¾ oz fresh lime juice

1 dash Abbotts bitters

orange zest, to garnish

SERVES 1

Add all the ingredients to a cocktail shaker, fill it with cubed ice, and shake hard for around 10 seconds. Strain into a pre-chilled cocktail glass and garnish with a coin of fresh orange zest, snapped over the drink and then discarded.

CHAPTER 5

UMAMI
Cocktails

Salt, sweet, bitter and sour have long been recognized as our four primary tastes but it wasn't until 1985 that the western world finally agreed with the east that there was a fifth, umami, the category of taste in food relative to the presence of glutamates, especially monosodium glutamate, a naturally abundant non-essential amino acid. Marmite, tomatoes, avocado, slow-cooked beef, mushrooms, soy, potatoes, sweetcorn, shellfish, green tea, carrots, tuna and Parmesan cheese are just some examples of food where umami is bountiful, with its rich, savoury, meaty like flavour. Derived from the Japanese word for delicious, 'umai', it's easy to understand why we have an obsession for umami-linked flavours.

The reason you love splashing soy sauce over the top of a plate of noodles, grating fresh Parmesan over pasta, splashing ketchup on top of your cheeseburger, or biting into whole cherry tomatoes in a salad? Umami. It's hard to describe the flavour we crave, but you know when it's not there. Similarly to salt, umami is a suppressor of bitterness and helps to accentuate the other primary tastes, however umami can be put to good use in tandem with bitter-heavy products to highlight other flavours away from the specific sensation of bitterness.

Bloody Mary (Improved)

Cocktail by Fernand Petiot

New York Bar, Paris, France

Spiced · Salt · Savoury

As with cups of tea, coffee or, more importantly in the case of this book, the martini, the bloody Mary is a very personal drink so there's not much you can do to mess it up other than shaking it. Never shake it. Simply start by combining vodka with a good-quality tomato juice and then add flavourings as you see fit. A general rule of thumb from all the outstanding variants I've tried is to incorporate ingredients that represent the five tastes of bitter, sweet, sour, salt and umami.

60 ml/2 oz Ketel One vodka

120 ml/4 oz tomato juice

15 ml/½ oz fresh lemon juice

3 dashes Bitter End Memphis barbecue bitters

4 dashes Worcestershire sauce

2 dashes Tabasco sauce

pinch of black pepper

pinch of celery salt

5 ml/1 teaspoon horseradish or English mustard

a pickled onion and freshly ground black pepper, to garnish

SERVES 1

Add all the ingredients to a cocktail shaker, fill it with cubed ice, and place a strainer over the ice to hold it back before pouring into an empty cocktail shaker. Pour the liquid back into the iced shaker and repeat this process 4–5 times to chill and dilute. Pour the finished drink over fresh ice in a highball glass and garnish with a pickled onion and a grind of black pepper.

Celery Sour

Cocktail by Jason Scott

Bramble, Edinburgh, Scotland

Bright · Citrus · Vegetal

This drink was one of the first cocktails I tried with celery bitters after they were released and it still ranks as one of the best cocktails I've ever tried. The crisp refreshing gin, sharp citrus bite of lemon, tart sweetness of fresh pineapple juice, and the velvety egg white texture makes for a tasty gin sour in its own right, but the addition of the bitters is magical, adding subtle hints of warm ginger, complex citrus and spiced vegetal notes from celery seed.

60 ml/2 oz dry gin or Everleaf Marine (alcohol-free)

30 ml/1 oz fresh lemon juice

15 ml/½ oz freshly pressed pineapple juice

15 ml/½ oz Cane Sugar Syrup *(see page 162)*

5 ml/1 teaspoon celery bitters

15 ml/½ oz fresh egg white

a ribbon of celery, to garnish

SERVES 1

Add all the ingredients to a cocktail shaker, fill it with cubed ice, and shake hard for around 10 seconds. Strain into a pre-chilled coupe glass and garnish with a strip of celery peeled using a potato peeler.

Oaxaca Old Fashioned

Cocktail by Phil Ward

Death & Co., New York City, USA

Oak · Spiced · Bittersweet

If there's any drink that's opened up people's eyes to the potential of mezcal in mixed drinks, this is it. Though many have dabbled with riffs on the Tequila Old Fashioned, this was the first I can recall seeing which combined the sweeter, drier, fruitier tequila with the complex leather, coffee, chilli, smoke, vanilla and spice of mezcals. Agave nectar adds just the right level of sweetness to round off the edges and intensify the flavours, whilst mole bitters will rarely find a better home with the spicy cacao and cinnamon offering length to the drink.

45 ml/1½ oz Reposado tequila

15 ml/½ oz mezcal

2 dashes Xocolatl mole bitters

5 ml/1 teaspoon agave nectar

fresh orange zest, to garnish

SERVES 1

Add all the ingredients to a mixing vessel, fill it with cubed ice, and briskly stir for around 15–20 seconds. Strain into an ice-filled rocks glass and garnish with a coin of fresh orange zest snapped over and dropped into the drink.

English Milk Punch

Cocktail by Daride Segat

Punch Room at The Edition Hotel, London, UK

Aromatic · Spiced · Complex

'What's going on here?' I hear you ask. Bromelain, an enzyme found in pineapple, breaks down casein, the proteins found in milk, leaving behind the texture and mouthfeel of milk but none of the colour.

If just one person goes to the effort of making this punch then my work here is done. Trust me, it's more than worth it. There's a reason it's gaining global popularity a few hundred years after it was originally created.

1 fresh pineapple

6 cloves

20 coriander seeds

1 stick of cinnamon

240 ml/8 oz fresh lemon juice

zest of 2 lemons

450 g/1 lb unrefined caster/superfine sugar

Peel and slice the pineapple into small chunks, then press with a rolling pin into the base of a vessel large enough to hold 6 litres/6⅓ quarts of liquid to extract all the juice. Grind the cloves, coriander seeds, and cinnamon stick, and add to the vessel.

Carefully grate the zest of two lemons, taking off as little pith as possible, then squeeze the lemons along with another four lemons to give you around 180 ml/6 oz of fresh lemon juice. Add this to the ground spices and pressed pineapple.

Add the sugar and stir until it has dissolved. Add the Cognac, rum, arrack, bitters, and tea, and stir thoroughly. Add the freshly boiled water, stir well, then cover and leave to macerate for no less than 6 hours.

After 6 hours, add the hot milk and squeeze another 2 oz/60 ml of fresh lemon juice, stir to combine, then allow to rest for 5 minutes or until the milk has curdled.

600 ml/20 oz brandy or Cognac

300 ml/10 oz aged rum

300 ml/10 oz Demerara rum

150 ml/5 oz arrack

30 ml/1 oz Dr. Adam's teapot bitters

240 ml/8 oz strong green tea

1.2 litres/40 oz freshly boiled water

1.2 litres/40 oz hot milk

Your punch now requires a two-step filtration. For the *first*, pour the liquid and solids through a fine-mesh sieve/strainer to extract large debris; repeat if necessary until all large debris has been removed. Allow to rest for a further 5 minutes and refrigerate if possible to allow the finer debris to rest at the base of your vessel.

For the *second* filtration, pour the liquid and fine sediment through a jelly bag to remove all the fine sediment. You may need to repeat this process until the liquid is clear.

To finish, bottle the liquid in clean, sterilized* glass bottles and keep refrigerated. It should store for around a month in your fridge.

To serve, pour the punch over a large block of ice in a punch bowl garnished with seasonal fruits, berries, spices and herbs. For individual serves, pour over ice in a small wine glass, tea cup or goblet.

*To sterilize a bottle, wash the glass and lid in hot, soapy water and place upside-down in a 120°C/ 250°F/Gas ½ oven to dry for 30 minutes, then remove.

B. F. G

Author's own

Rich · Fruit · Smoked

Another of those hybrid drinks that just make sense, this time a combination of two of the most famous Scotch whisky cocktails, the Rob Roy (Scotch whisky, vermouth, bitters) and the rusty nail (Scotch whisky and Drambuie). The name is a nod to the first recorded reference of a drink combining whisky and Drambuie, the B.I.F from 1937, which was named for the British Industries Fair held annually in Birmingham from the 1920s until the mid 20th century.

45 ml/1½ oz Drambuie

22.5 ml/¾ oz Italian (sweet) vermouth

10 ml/⅓ oz Laphroaig 10 year old

2 dashes Dr. Adam's Boker's bitters

lemon zest, to garnish

SERVES 1

Add all the ingredients to a mixing vessel, fill it with cubed ice, and briskly stir for around 15–20 seconds. Strain into a pre-chilled cocktail glass and garnish with a coin of fresh lemon zest snapped over and dropped into the drink.

Mayas Daiquiri

Cocktail by David Cordoba

Bramble, Edinburgh, Scotland

Fresh · Green · Moreish

A twist on the classic daiquiri (rum, lime and sugar) inspired by an avocado and sugar pure David's grandmother used to treat him to. In lieu of the drier light rum traditionally used in daiquiris, the drink utilizes and aged rum that has pronounced notes of coffee, chocolate, toffee and caramel, all of which partner wonderfully with avocado. The drink further swaps out sugar for honey-like agave nectar, with fresh lime providing balance, freshness and my addition of cardamom bitters adding further length and depth.

½ fresh ripe avocado

60 ml/2 oz aged rum

1 dash cardamom bitters

15 ml/½ oz fresh lime juice

22.5 ml/¾ oz agave syrup

a pineapple frond, to garnish

SERVES 1

Peel and chop the avocado, then add it to the base of a cocktail shaker and muddle into a purée. Add the remaining ingredients, stir to combine, then fill with cubed ice and shake hard for around 10 seconds. Strain into a pre-chilled coupe glass and garnish with a pineapple frond.

Adonis Cocktail

Unknown

Waldorf-Astoria Hotel, New York City, USA

Dried fruit · Spice · Bittersweet

Not too dissimilar to the make-up of the martini (gin, vermouth, bitters), the Adonis is an old-timey, aromatic cocktail which is great before or after dinner, and especially so as an accompaniment to a cheeseboard. The base spirit of oloroso sherry, big on umami and with a dried fruit, spice and leather flavour profile, perfectly complements the dark fruits and berries in sweet vermouth. (*pictured on page 138*)

45 ml/1½ oz dry oloroso sherry

45 ml/1½ oz Italian (sweet) vermouth

2 dashes Dr. Adam's Spanish bitters or orange bitters

a slice of orange, to garnish

SERVES 1

Add all the ingredients to your mixing vessel, fill it with cubed ice, and briskly stir for around 15–20 seconds. Strain into a pre-chilled cocktail glass and garnish with a slice of orange cut into a quarter, rubbed around the rim of the glass, then dropped into the drink.

Bamboo

Cocktail by Louis Eppinger

Grand Hotel, Yokohama, Japan

Dry · Mineral · Complex

Turning the Adonis on its head by replacing the nutty, spicy oloroso sherry and sweet, fruity vermouth, Eppinger would employ the dry, acidic fino sherry and the soft fruit, crisp and floral notes from the dry vermouth. To lend balance and length, I suggest reaching for an orange bitters that leans toward a sweeter, candied orange profile, in tandem with the spiced aromatic bitters. *(pictured on page 138)*

45 ml/1½ oz fino sherry

45 ml/1½ oz French (dry) vermouth

1 dash Dr. Adam's Spanish bitters or orange bitters

1 dash aromatic bitters (Angostura, Bitter Truth Old Time, or Orinoco)

a slice of lemon, to garnish

SERVES 1

Add all the ingredients to a mixing vessel, fill it with cubed ice, and briskly stir for around 15–20 seconds. Strain into a pre-chilled cocktail glass and garnish with a slice of lemon cut into a quarter, rubbed around the rim of the glass, then dropped into the drink.

Autumn Negroni

Cocktail by Danny Whelan

Kelvingrove Cafe, Glasgow, Scotland

Dry · Earthy · Bittersweet

As far as fool-proof recipes go the negroni has them all beat. The Autumn negroni infuses sweet vermouth with dried porcini mushrooms, adding an incredible earthy, woody and nutty character that pairs wonderfully with spicy, bitter orange Campari, the dry, fresh gin, and the warm lemony-citrus coriander bitters rounding things off.

30 ml/1 oz **The House of Botanicals ABZ dry gin**

30 ml/1 oz **Campari**

30 ml/1 oz **Italian (sweet) vermouth infused with porcini mushroom** *(see page 160)*

1 dash **coriander bitters**

a dried lemon wheel, to garnish

SERVES 1

Add all the ingredients to a mixing vessel, fill it with cubed ice, and briskly stir for around 15–20 seconds. Strain into an ice-filled rocks glass and garnish with a dried lemon wheel.

Hong Kong Brunch

Cocktail by Patrick Noir

M.V.P., Dublin, Ireland

Fresh · Tropical · Herbal

Even now when I look at this recipe it doesn't make sense, but it's not until you remove the associated names and focus on the flavours contained within that it all comes together; the fresh, orange-heavy gin pairing wonderfully with the stoned fruit of the Cognac, the tart refreshing aspect of pineapple and lime juices working in harmony with the tea syrup, and the herbaceous, spiced absinthe and bitters adding backbone with hints of liquorice and anise.

30 ml/1 oz Beefeater 24 dry gin

30 ml/1 oz brandy or Cognac

22.5 ml/¾ oz freshly pressed pineapple juice

10 ml/⅓ oz fresh lime juice

10 ml/⅓ oz Lapsang Souchong Syrup *(see page 164)*

1 dash absinthe

2 dashes Peychaud's bitters

a pineapple frond, to garnish

SERVES 1

Add all the ingredients to a cocktail shaker, fill it with cubed ice, and shake hard for around 10 seconds. Strain into an ice-filled highball glass and garnish with a pineapple frond.

CHAPTER 6

BASIC
Recipes

In the following pages you will find basic recipes for making various syrups, simple infusions and tinctures that will elevate the quality of the drinks you make at home. These are used in cocktails featured in the recipe sections, each being crucial to the specific recipe where they are utilized.

Check the list of the ingredients for the drink you plan to make first, then visit this section to find a simple recipe with instructions. I guarantee you will find the time it takes to make each one is worth the effort when you take your first sip of the resulting, perfectly balanced drink.

Jasmine Tea-infused Vodka

1 jasmine tea bag

700 ml/23 oz/ 2¾ cups vodka

Combine both the tea and spirit in a clean jar, stir thoroughly and allow to rest for 30 minutes. Remove the teabag and squeeze to extract all liquid. Using a funnel, pour back into the empty vodka bottle, seal and label. This will keep indefinitely.

Porcini-infused Vermouth

15 g/½ oz dried porcini mushrooms

700 ml/23 oz/ 2¾ cups Cocchi Vermouth di Torino

Roughly chop the mushrooms then combine with the vermouth in a clean jar, stir thoroughly and allow to rest for 2 weeks, agitating daily. Strain through coffee filter paper then, using a funnel, pour back into the empty vermouth bottle, seal, label and refrigerate. This will keep for 4 weeks.

Pandan-infused Tawny Port

8 pandan leaves

**700 ml/23 oz/
2¾ cups tawny port**

Roughly chop the pandan leaves then combine with the port in a clean jar, stir thoroughly and allow to rest for 1 week, agitating daily. Strain through coffee filter paper then, using a funnel, pour back into the empty port bottle, seal, label and refrigerate. Will keep for 4 weeks.

Demerara Sugar Syrup

600 g/20 oz/3 cups Demerara sugar

300 ml/10 oz/ 1 ¼ cups water

Combine the sugar and water in a suitable mixing vessel and stir vigorously until the sugar has fully dissolved. Using a funnel, pour into clean, glass bottles, then seal, label and refrigerate. Will keep for up to 4 weeks.

Tip: If using granulated sugar you can aid the process of dissolving by grinding the sugar to a finer powder using a food processor.

Cane Sugar Syrup

600 g/20 oz/3 cups unrefined cane sugar

300 ml/10 oz/ 1¼ cups water

Combine the sugar and water in a suitable mixing vessel and stir vigorously until the sugar has fully dissolved. Using a funnel, pour into clean glass bottles, then seal, label and refrigerate. Will keep for up to 4 weeks.

Tip: If using granulated sugar you can aid the process of dissolving by grinding the sugar to a finer powder using a food processor.

Vanilla Sugar Syrup

1 vanilla pod/bean

600 g/20 oz/3 cups
unrefined cane sugar

300 ml/10 oz/
1¼ cups water

Score the vanilla pod and add to the sugar, agitate thoroughly and allow to rest for at least 1 week before using. Combine the vanilla-infused sugar and water in a suitable mixing vessel and stir vigorously until the sugar has fully dissolved. Using a funnel, pour into clean, glass bottles, then seal, label and refrigerate. Will keep for up to 4 weeks.

Tip: If using granulated sugar you can aid the process of dissolving by grinding the sugar to a finer powder using a food processor.

Pineapple Syrup

1 pineapple

600 g/20 oz/3 cups
unrefined cane sugar

300 ml/10 oz/
1¼ cups water

Peel the pineapple and cut into cubes. Using a citrus press, squeeze the pineapple cubes to extract all juice, also adding the squeezed pulp. Combine with the sugar and water in a suitable mixing vessel and stir vigorously until the sugar has fully dissolved. Allow to rest for 24 hours before straining through a fine mesh sieve/strainer. Using a funnel, pour into clean, glass bottles, then seal, label and refrigerate. Will keep for up to 4 weeks.

Tip: If using granulated sugar you can aid the process of dissolving by grinding the sugar to a finer powder using a food processor.

Gunpowder Tea Syrup

20 ml/⅔ oz
Gunpowder Tea
Tincture (see right)

680 ml/22½ oz Cane
Sugar Syrup *(see
page 162)*

Combine the tincture and syrup in a suitable mixing vessel and stir until fully combined. Using a funnel, pour into clean, glass bottles, then seal, label and refrigerate. Will keep for up to 4 weeks.

Lapsang Souchong Syrup

600 g/20 oz/3 cups
unrefined cane sugar

300 ml/10 oz/
1¼ cups strong
brewed Lapsang
Souchong tea

Combine the sugar and tea in a suitable mixing vessel and stir vigorously until the sugar has fully dissolved. Using a funnel, pour into clean, glass bottles, then seal, label and refrigerate. Will keep for up to 4 weeks.

Tip: If using granulated sugar you can aid the process of dissolving by grinding the sugar to a finer powder using a food processor.

Gunpowder Tea Tincture

30 g/1 oz gunpowder tea

150 ml/5 oz/⅔ cup 96% ABV neutral spirit

150 ml/5 oz/⅔ cup water

Combine both the tea and spirit in a clean jar, stir thoroughly and allow to rest for 2 days. Strain through coffee filter paper then add the water. Using a funnel, pour into a clean dasher bottle. Will keep indefinitely.

Note: This is approximately 45—48% abv.

Mace Tincture

30 g/1 oz freshly ground mace blades

150 ml/5 oz/⅔ cup 96% ABV neutral spirit

150 ml/5 oz/⅔ cup water

Combine both the mace and spirit in a clean jar, stir thoroughly and allow to rest for 5 days. Strain through coffee filter paper then add the water. Using a funnel, pour into a clean dasher bottle. Will keep indefinitely.

Note: This is approximately 45—48% abv.

Lemon Sherbet

6 unwaxed lemons

600 g/20 oz/3 cups
unrefined cane sugar

540 ml/18 oz/
2¼ cups fresh lemon
juice

Using a vegetable peeler remove the zest from
the lemon, leaving behind as much pith as
possible, and combine with the sugar. Agitate
thoroughly with your hands to ensure the oils of
the zest and sugar have fully integrated and rest
for 24 hours. Add the fresh lemon juice and stir
until dissolved. Strain through a fine mesh sieve/
strainer, then funnel into a clean, glass bottle and
refrigerate. Will keep for 3 days.

Grapefruit & Cardamom Sherbet

3 ruby grapefruits

4 green cardamom pods

600 g/20 oz/3 cups unrefined cane sugar

270 ml/9 oz/scant 1¼ cups fresh ruby grapefruit juice

270 ml/9 oz/scant 1¼ cups fresh lemon juice

Using a vegetable peeler remove the zest from the grapefruit, leaving behind as much pith as possible, and combine with the sugar along with crushed cardamom pods. Agitate thoroughly with your hands to ensure the oils of the zest, cardamom and sugar have fully integrated and rest for 24 hours. Add the fresh grapefruit and lemon juice and stir until dissolved. Strain through a fine mesh sieve/strainer, then funnel into a clean, glass bottle and refrigerate. Will keep for 3 days.

Kosher Salt, Celery Salt, & Sugar Mix

30 g/1 oz Kosher salt

30 g/1 oz celery salt

30 g/1 oz unrefined cane sugar

Combine all the ingredients and mix thoroughly. Store in a clean jar in a cool, dry place. This will keep indefinitely.

Vanilla Salt

1 vanilla bean/pod

240 g/9 oz/1¼ cups table salt

Score the vanilla pod and add to the salt, agitate thoroughly and allow to rest for at least 1 week before using. Store in a cool, dry place. This will keep indefinitely.

Saline Solution

30 g/1 oz table salt

300 ml/10 oz/ 1¼ cups water

Combine the salt and water in a suitable mixing vessel and stir vigorously until the salt has fully dissolved. Using a funnel, pour into a clean dasher bottle. Will keep indefinitely.

Ingredient Glossary

The following is a concise snapshot of all the bitters featured in the cocktail recipes section. This glossary identifies the key botanicals and flavourings associated with each bitters and can be used to determine the specific tastes they offer, while providing an idea of what to use as a substitute should the original bottling be unavailable.

Amargo Chuncho Bitters

(Peru – 40% ABV):

Baking spices, bittersweet, aromatic

Angostura Aromatic Bitters

(Trinidad & Tobago – 44.7% ABV):

Warm spice, cherry, cola

Angostura Orange Bitters

(Trinidad & Tobago – 28% ABV):

Candied orange, spice, coriander

Bitter End Memphis Barbecue Bitters

(USA – 45% ABV):

Smoke, chipotle, spice

Bitter Truth Celery Bitters

(Germany – 44% ABV):

Celery, lemongrass, ginger

Bitter Truth Old Time Bitters

(Germany – 39% ABV):

Clove, gingerbread, cardamom

Bittermens Hopped Grapefruit Bitters

(USA – 53% ABV):

Bitter grapefruit, pine, citrus

Bittermens Xocolatl Mole Bitters

(USA – 53% ABV):

Bitter chocolate, black pepper, rich

Bob's Abbotts Bitters

(England – 41.8% ABV):

Herbal, spicy, bitter

Bob's Coriander Bitters

(England – 30% ABV):

Vegetal, coriander, bittersweet

Dale DeGroff's Pimento Bitters

(France – 45% ABV):

Clove, licorice, warm spices

Dr. Adam's Aphrodite Bitters

(Scotland – 38% ABV):

Cacao, coffee, chili

Dr. Adam's Boker's Bitters

(Scotland – 31.5% ABV):

Cardamom, citrus, bitter coffee

Dr. Adam's Dandelion & Burdock Bitters

(Scotland – 42% ABV):

Licorice, spice, earthy

Dr. Adam's Orinoco Aromatic Bitters

(Scotland – 45% ABV):

Baking spice, bittersweet, molasses

Dr. Adam's Spanish Bitters

(Scotland – 38% ABV):

Floral, citrus, marmalade

Dr. Adam's Teapot Bitters

(Scotland – 38% ABV):

Black tea, vanilla, baking spice

Peychaud's Bitters

(USA – 35% ABV):

Anise, spice, stoned fruit

Regans' Orange No. 6 Bitters

(USA – 45% ABV):

Bitter orange, cardamom, spice

Scrappy's Cardamom Bitters

(USA – 52% ABV):

Sweet, cardamom, citrus

Index

About the Author

Adam Elan-Elmegirab is a former bartender and founder of The House of Botanicals in Aberdeen, producing three brands of The House of Botanical Gins, Dr. Adam's Cocktail Bitters and Pietro Nicola Aperitivi & Digestivo. When not knee-deep in botanicals, Adam travels extensively, writes for a number of drinks media publications, is a former judge for two world bar award shows, collaborates with a number of bars and brands, and regularly presents seminars and tastings at international cocktail events.

Acknowledgments

Though I'll be given all the credit as the author of this book, the lessons, learnings and experiences that have shaped who I am and what I do now in my career go right back to the day I was born so it's impossible to list everyone who has, both directly and indirectly, impacted this work. First of all a huge thanks to Julia and the team at Ryland Peters & Small for approaching and trusting me to work on this updated edition. Thank you to all the bartenders, bars, retailers, wholesalers and distributors across the world for supporting the endeavours of our small family operation at The House of Botanicals. To my mum, Rami, Cherie, Danielle, Nicole, Sarah, Olivia, Sam, Campbell, Conor, Moira and Jim for always being there for me despite the fact I can never seem to switch off from work. To Margaux for being the most incredible companion 🐾.To my stunning wife Steffie who has to deal with me every day and constantly supports what I endeavour to do. You're our rock. To my beautiful daughter Saffron. Everything I do is for you. And lastly to my younger brother Aimin, the best of us taken too soon. Every day I take a walk down memory lane so I can bump into you. We'll keep your flag flying high.

Picture credits:
Cover illustration: Adobestock.com 526996011 by Olga Miraniuk; cover photograph: Adobestock.com 427165426 by laplateresca; illustrations: Abigail Read; pages 5, 29, 30, 31, 33, 34, 35, 56–157 photography Terry Benson, styling Kim Sullivan; pages 2, 6, 9, 19, 41, 42, 49, 50, 53, 55, 158 photography Catherine Gratwicke, styling Emily Henson; page 17 William Lingwood; page 19 Kim Lightbody; page 26 Dr. Adam Elmegirab's Bitters; page 45 Adrian Lawrence; page 46 Gavin Kingscombe; page 129 Callooh Callay Bar.